MYSTERIOUS SITES IN THE LANDSCAPE

MEGALITHS OF WALES

CHRIS BARBER

In memory of my friend John G. Williams, who had a lifelong interest in megalithic monuments and extraordinary abilities as a dowser.

The ancient people who built the megalithic structures were clearly involved in something practical as well as sacred, and that practice gave them a very special, mysterious relationship with the Earth.

Paul Devereux

Front Cover: St Lythans Cromlech, Glamorgan.

First published by Blorenge Book.
This edition published by Amberley Publishing, 2017.

Amberley Publishing
The Hill, Stroud
Gloucestershire, GL5 4EP

www.amberley-books.com

Copyright © Chris Barber 2017

The right of Chris Barber to be identified as the Author of this work has been asserted in accordance with the Copyright, Designs and Patents Act 1988.

All rights reserved. No part of this book may be reprinted or reproduced or utilised in any form or by any electronic, mechanical or other means, now known or hereafter invented, including photocopying and recording, or in any information storage or retrieval system, without the permission in writing from the Publishers.

British Library Cataloguing in Publication Data.
A catalogue record for this book is available from the British Library.

ISBN 978 1 4456 7400 1 (paperback)
ISBN 978 1 4456 7401 8 (ebook)

Origination by Amberley Publishing.

Acknowledgements

This book is the result of explorations over many years and I am grateful to landowners who gave me access to some of the monuments on private land and various people who sometimes pointed me in the right direction when seeking certain elusive megalithic monuments.

I give special thanks to my wife Anne Marie who accompanied me on many of my journeys around Wales during the last decade and not only shared my enthusiasm for these enigmatic stones, but also made invaluable suggestions for improving my manuscript.

Finally, my gratitude is also due to the staff at Amberley Publishing for producing this book and it has been a pleasure to work with them.

The author inspecting a megalithic site in Carmarthenshire.

Contents

	Preface	7
	Guidelines	8

PART ONE

Chapter 1	Standing Stones	11
Chapter 2	Stone Rows	35
Chapter 3	Stone Circles	43
Chapter 4	Cromlechs and Dolmens	57
Chapter 5	Gallery Graves, Long Cairns and Chambered Tombs	77
Chapter 6	Misconceptions and Preconceived Ideas	91
Chapter 7	Markings on the Stones	95
Chapter 8	Churches Built on Megalithic Sites	111
Chapter 9	Some Fascinating Legends	115
Chapter 10	Astronomical Significance	149
Chapter 11	The Destruction of Megalithic Monuments	153

PART TWO: ALTERNATIVE ARCHAEOLOGY 159

Chapter 12	Ley Lines and Scemb Lines	161
Chapter 13	Dowsing the Earth Energies	167
Chapter 14	Fogging of Photographs	175
Chapter 15	The Significance of Quartz	179
Chapter 16	Some Interesting and Intriguing Facts	181
Chapter 17	Assorted Theories	184
	Glossary of Terms	188
	Further Reading	191
	Other Books by Chris Barber	192

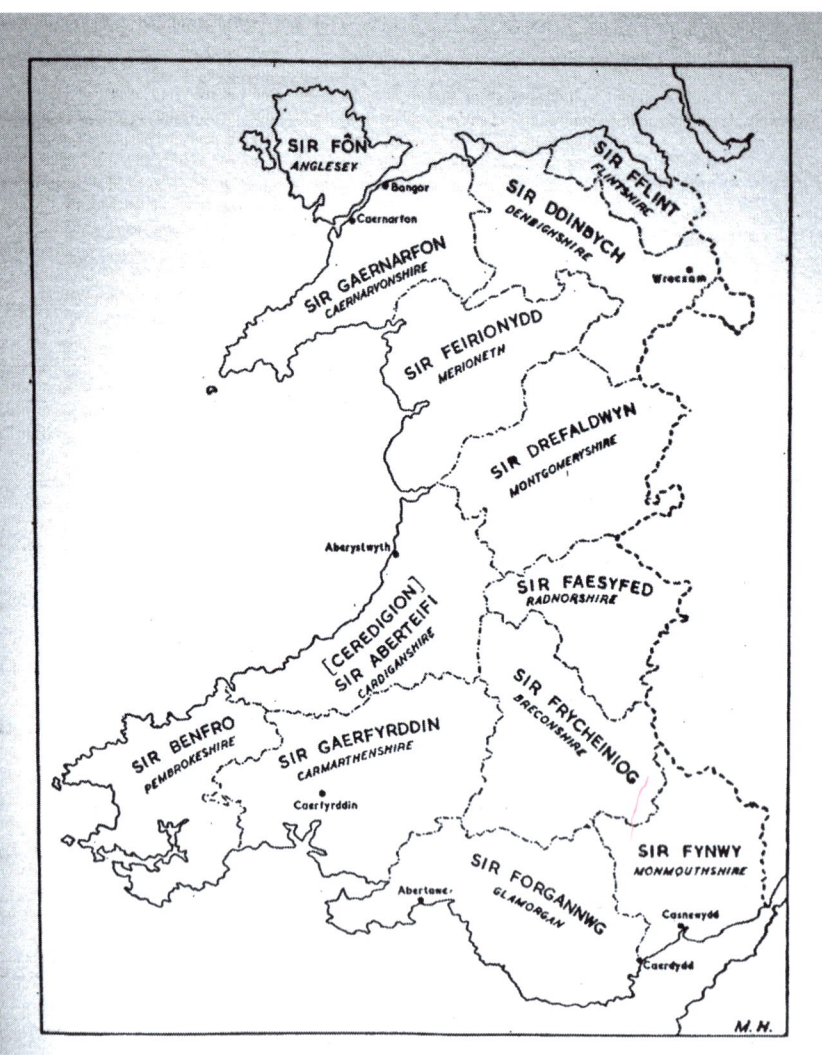

Siroedd Cymru

The Counties of Wales

Preface

In 1989 I published a book entitled *The Ancient Stones of Wales*, which I wrote in conjunction with the late John Godfrey Williams, who was a retired solicitor and a well-known dowser with extraordinary powers. We decided to combine our knowledge, gained from many years of independent research, to produce a book relating to the prehistoric monuments of Wales.

Four thousand copies of our book were sold and it has now been out of print since the year 2000. During the last two decades I have undertaken further research into the subject, and as the previous book is now much sought after by those interested in megalithic monuments, I have decided to bring out a new book on this subject, which, like the original one, relates entirely to Wales.

You have to be a walker with good map and compass skills in order to ascend windswept hillsides or cross extensive moorland to find sites in remote locations. The megalithic monument that you seek may often be in some lonely intriguing place where the spirit of the past lingers on. When visiting these sites one should try to tune in to our distant ancestors and ponder on their purpose in erecting these ancient monuments, which due to their size and construction are often quite remarkable and represent prehistoric riddles waiting to be solved.

These monuments were erected up to four thousand years ago during a time when man must have felt closer to nature and it is my hope that on reading this book, you will feel compelled to go in search of these mysterious megaliths to ponder on their purpose.

Chris Barber
Llanfoist 2017

Guidelines

Maps
Wales is covered by twenty-three maps in the Ordnance Survey 1:50,000 series. For greater detail 1:25,000 scale maps may be used, but six times the number are required to cover the same area, which would prove expensive for the casual visitor.

Grid References
The locations of the sites are given as six-figure grid references; for example SJ 172679 (116). The letters at the beginning of the six-figure reference can be ignored as long as the correct map is used. The relevant Ordnance Survey 1:50,000 map number is given in brackets after the grid reference to enable the reader to identify the appropriate map easily. The letters at the beginning of the six-figure reference can be ignored if the correct map is used.

Reading a Grid Reference
Ordnance Survey maps are divided into 1-kilometre squares formed by imaginary lines, which are numbered in the map margins. To find a map reference such as 687694, do the following:

(1) Look along the northern margin of the map for no. 68 and then divide the area between 68 and 69 into ten imaginary sections, each one-tenth of a kilometre apart. Continue eastwards beyond 68 for seven-tenths of the distance to 69.
(2) Look up the eastern margin of the map for no. 69 and then divide the area between 69 and 70 into ten imaginary sections, each again one-tenth of a kilometre apart. Continue northwards beyond 69 for four-tenths of the distance to 70.

Guidelines

(3) We now have two points on the margins of the map: 68 – 7 on the northern margin and 69 – 4 on the eastern margin. Where imaginary lines are drawn through these points parallel to the printed lines, the point at which they intersect is the map reference.

Names of Counties
The historic names for counties have been used instead of the confusing modern names of local authority administrations, which are likely to change with yet another reorganisation proposed at the time of writing.

Be Prepared
When visiting sites in remote moorland and hill country be sure to wear sensible footwear and take waterproof clothing. A compass and the ability to use it is also advisable.

Access
Please note: Do not assume automatic right of access to any site. Most of them are accessible, being on common land, but some stand on private property. In these instances one should always seek the landowner's permission to cross their land. They are generally very co-operative and will often give you directions to the site of the monument. Always keep to the edge of fields, avoid damaging crops and always leave gates as you find them.

Spelling of Place Names
Generally, the Ordnance Survey spelling of place names has been used to assist the reader with identification of sites on the map.

Measurements
Instead of giving both metric and imperial measurements for the monuments, I have just used yards, feet and inches, which is my personal preference, and have left it to the reader to convert them to metric if so wished.

Selection of Sites
This book includes examples of interesting sites that can be visited in various parts of Wales, but they only represent a very small percentage of the large number of megaliths that exist in Wales. Others can be identified by Ordnance Survey maps. It is hoped that these examples will inspire further exploration.

Megaliths of Wales: Mysterious Sites in the Landscape

Cerrig Meibion Arthur, Pembrokeshire.

PART ONE

I

Standing Stones

A standing stone embedded in the earth, is in mute communion with the harsh inorganic world of its birth.

Don Robins

The word 'megalith' was invented by an Oxford don, Algernon Herbert, in 1849, for use in his book *Cyclops Christianus*. He anglicised the two Greek words *mega* (big) and *llithos* (stone) and it means any massive stone but generally refers to a standing stone of the Neolithic period. One can come across these enigmatic monuments in many parts of Britain, but also throughout the world, in places such as Asia, Japan, Korea, India, Iran, Syria, along the north coast of Africa from Tripoli to Morocco, the Caucasus, the Crimea, Bulgaria, Sweden, Denmark and Europe.

They were obviously erected for a purpose and there are numerous theories to be found in the wide assortment of books that have been written on this intriguing subject. For example, were the solitary standing stones erected as route markers on ancient trackways, or as burial markers, commemorating persons of importance in prehistoric times? Some people also believe that the megalithic sites mark places of power where little-understood energies or forces were gathered together and directed for some long-forgotten purpose.

Single standing stones are usually found in isolation, but sometimes they occur in groups of two or three and nearly all of them can be said to be of the pillar type, with a roughly rectangular section at the point where they protrude from the ground. They are found in all shapes and sizes and vary in height above the level of the ground from about 2 feet to over 18 feet, such as the tallest standing stone in Wales, the Fish Stone (*see* page 15).

Megaliths of Wales: Mysterious Sites in the Landscape

The largest known standing stone in the world is Le Grand Menhir Brisé at Locmariaquer, near Carnac in Brittany. It now lies on the ground broken into four pieces, but once stood 57 feet high, weighed about 380 tons and could be seen from 10 miles out at sea and was perhaps used as a distant foresight from which moon eclipses could be predicted. This huge stone may have fallen during an earthquake in 1722 and it is of a variety of granite of which the nearest outcrop is 80km away in Finistére.

Standing Stones often taper upwards to a cone or a point and it is possible that they may have had definite shapes when they were erected thousands of years ago, but constant wind and rain have obscured any real signs of this, and they are generally regarded as shapeless lumps of erect rock by most people. Although looking rough and unhewn, the stones may well have been roughly carved into shapes that were considered convenient, or even perhaps necessary. Also, they must have been worked on by some kind of tools to separate them from their place of origin, which is often a considerable distance from the spot in which they have been erected.

Excavations that have been undertaken at single standing stones have shown that about one third of the total height of the stone is buried in the ground. This means that if you look at a standing stone that is 6 feet above ground level, then there is likely to be at least 3 feet of the stone below the surface. If the proportion was less, then the megalith would be top-heavy and could be made to fall over without much effort. It is amazing to consider how many of these prehistoric standing stones are still very firmly embedded in the ground, and it is a tribute to the builders, who knew exactly what they were doing four or five thousand years ago.

One might imagine that a single standing stone marks the site of an important burial, perhaps of some local chief, but archaeological excavation reports show little evidence to support this idea. Even when human remains have been found at the foot of these stone pillars, it is usually ashes of the burnt human bones and there is nothing to indicate that these were placed in the ground at the time of the erection of the stone.

Megaliths cannot be dated accurately because radiocarbon dating works only with matter that has been alive, so the stones can only be dated using techniques on organic matter that can be assumed to have been associated with the erection of the structure. Carbon dating of burial remains found at the foot of some British standing stones suggest they were erected about 2,000 BC.

Llwyn-y-Fedwen Stone.

A Tall Standing Stone
Llwyn-y-Fedwen Stone is situated within a hedge boundary near the north bank of the River Usk, to the north of Llangynidr village. Composed of erratic limestone and leaning slightly to the north, it is 14 feet high by 4 feet square and is estimated to weigh about 20 tons. There is a large horizontal crack and a blackened patch near its base.

Location: East of the B4560 on private land, near the River Usk, Brecknockshire – SO 157204 (161)

The Tallest Standing Stone in West Wales
Hirfaen Gwyddog is also known as Carreg Hirfaen, and this 15-foot standing stone marks the boundary between the old counties of Carmarthenshire and Cardiganshire. There is a modern inscription on the stone.

Location: 5 miles south of Llanfair Clydogau B4343 and near Brynhirfaen, Carmarthenshire – SN 625464 (146)

Hirfaen Gwyddog.

Standing Stones

The Tallest Standing Stone in Wales
The Fish Stone which stands on the bank of the River Usk between Penmyarth and Llangynidr Bridge (private land) is the tallest standing stone in Wales. It is 18 feet high and resembles a huge salmon jumping vertically with its tail touching the ground. There is a vague sort of eye at the top or head of the stone and a 'fin' on the side facing the river. There is a local legend that on Midsummer Eve it jumps into the River Usk and goes for a swim.

The total height must be about 27 feet, if we assume that one third of its height (9 feet) is in the ground. This impressive stone stands at the top of a steep bank about 25 yards from the River Usk. It is composed of Old Red Sandstone and is believed to have been extracted from somewhere on the other side of the river. The erectors then hauled the stone up a steep bank and placed it in a large hole, which had been excavated to hold it upright.

Location: On the north bank of the River Usk between Penmyarth and Llangynidr Bridge, near Crickhowell, Brecknockshire – SO 183198 (161)

Please note: Permission to visit this site is needed from the Glen Usk Estate property manager.

The Fish Stone, Penmyarth.

Megaliths of Wales: Mysterious Sites in the Landscape

The Pentrefelin Stone.

The Thinnest Standing Stone in Wales

The Pentrefelin Stone is 10 feet high and has 12-inch sides. It is marked with a cross and bears the date '1721'. Originally it used to stand near the edge of a small pond, from which Pentrefelin (Mill Village) takes its name. The stone was moved to the present position in 1933 when the main road was widened.

Location: Beside the A497 between Porthmadog and Criccieth, in the village of Pentrefelin – SH 529397 (124)

Standing Stones

A large stone near the Usk Reservoir.

A Very Wide Standing Stone
In a boggy field is a large greyish stone about 7 feet high, which appears to have originally been a dark-reddish colour.

Location: Just south of the dam of Usk Reservoir, and near the Dwr Llydan brook, Brecknockshire – SN 834284 (160)

Maen Llwyd in the Black Mountains.

The Highest Standing Stone in Wales
Maen Llwyd (Grey Stone), which is situated at 1,880 feet above sea level, near the head of the Grwyne Fawr Valley in the Black Mountains, is claimed to be the highest standing stone in Wales. The stone is 7 feet tall and has large circular hollows on its sides.

Location: Near the head of the Grwyne Fechan valley on the upper southern slope of Pen y Gadair Fawr, in the Black Mountains, Brecknockshire – SO 226276 (161).

Standing Stones

Meini Hirion Stones.

A Triangle of Stones
Meini Hirion Stones is a triangular setting of three upright stones about 6½ feet in height. They are marked as Meini Hirion on Ordnance Survey maps.

Location: On Cromlech Farm between the village of Llanfechell and Foel Fawr, Anglesey – SH364917 (114)

Megaliths of Wales: Mysterious Sites in the Landscape

The Llanrhidian Stones.

Curiosities on the Village Green

The Llanrhidian Stones are two large megaliths which can be seen on the sloping village green either side of the path leading to Llanrhidian Church. The upper stone is a slab of quartz-conglomerate from Cefn Bryn and mounted on a limestone base; it is curiously shaped, with three short stumps sticking out of the top. It has been suggested that it is the remains of a tenth-century Celtic wheel cross. Iron staples were at one time embedded into the stone. The top could have been knocked off by Puritans during the Reformation and the staples inserted long afterwards, when the stone was used as a sort of village pillory. It is known locally as the 'Whipping Stone'.

The lower stone (SS 497922) is a block of limestone and when it was raised up in 1844 the event was recorded as follows in the Parish register:

> On the 8th day of April a very large stone weighing nearly two tons was raised on its end a short distance from the Welcome To Town public house; 10 to 12 men volunteered to do it – one pint each.

Location: Near Llanrhidian Church, Gower, Glamorgan – SS 497922 (159)

Standing Stones

A Pass Marked by Two Stones

Bwlch y Ddeufaen (pass of the two stones) is where two prehistoric standing stones stand either side of a Roman road crossing moorland on a route from the Conwy Valley to the coast. Bwlch y Ddeufaen is a mountain pass 1,400 feet above sea level on the old Roman road connecting Canovium (Caerhun) with Segontium (Caernarfon). The pointed stone is 9 feet tall while the other one stands at 6 feet.

Location: About 3 miles west of Rowen, below Foel Lwyd, Caernarfonshire – SC 716716 (115)

Hoary and lichened by age, grim and fretted by a thousand storms our ancient megalithic monuments are still numerous, massive and full of mystery.

Walter Johns

The two stones at Bwlch y Ddeufaen.

Megaliths of Wales: Mysterious Sites in the Landscape

Bedd Morris.

Used as a Boundary Marker
Bedd Morris is 6 feet 6 inches tall and tapers to a point. It was marked in the eighteenth century by a landowner who decided to use it as a boundary stone marking the limit of his property. In addition, there is an Ordnance Survey benchmark carved on the stone. A few years ago it was knocked over by a car and had to be re-erected. There is a car park opposite the stone.

Location: Positioned on the side of a minor road from Pontfaen to Newport, Pembrokeshire – SN 038366

Standing Stones

The Great Oak Stone.

Mistakenly Identified as a Boundary Stone
The Great Oak Stone, near Crickhowell, is also known as Llangenny Lane Standing Stone. It is just over 7 feet high, 5 feet 4 inches wide and 1 foot 6 inches thick. It appears as 'Stone' on the Ordnance Survey maps of 1831 and 1947, but in more recent years is marked as B.S., having been mistaken as merely a boundary marker. Dowsers have found that this megalith is of ideal height for detecting the 5th and 7th bands of power (see pages 172–173).

Location: In a field on the east side of Great Oak Road above Crickhowell, Brecknockshire – SO 223185 (161)

Please note: This stone is situated on private land and entry to the field is discouraged by barbed wire on the gate.

Megaliths of Wales: Mysterious Sites in the Landscape

Battle Stone.

Named after an Eleventh-Century Battle
Battle Stone is about 12 feet high and has a low mound on its north side. The stone takes its name from a battle that was fought in 1088 nearby between a Norman force led by Bernard de Newmarche and Rhys ap Tewdwr, King of South Wales who had come to the assistance of Bleddyn ap Maenarch, ruler of Brycheiniog. The Welshmen were defeated and killed and the battle was commemorated by the foundation of Battle Chapel, which is situated a short distance away.

Location: At the bottom of a steep slope from Battle Church, near a road and the old railway line from Brecon, Brecknockshire – SO 006306 (160)

Waen Lleuci.

An Interesting Alignment
Waen Lleuci is a large grey standing stone about 7 feet tall by 5 feet wide and less than 1 foot thick. It is composed of Old Red Sandstone and stands below the slopes of Moel Feity. In relationship to its size, this stone is very thin and it is aligned with a stone called Maen Mawr. The centre of Coed Duon Stone Circle (see page 48) and Saith Maen alignment is 3½ miles away.

Location: On access land to the east of the mountain road between Glyntawe and Trecastle. Brecknockshire – SN 854215 (160)

Megaliths of Wales: Mysterious Sites in the Landscape

The Bwlch Stone.

A Marker for the Bwlch Pass

The Bwlch Stone is about 5 feet 6 inches high and can be seen clearly from the road leading up to the summit of the pass at Bwlch. Over the years, animals in the field have found this stone useful as a 'rubbing' post.

Location: In a field (private farmland) to the west of the A40. Below the village of Bwlch, Brecknockshire – SO 150219 (161).

Standing Stones

The Pumsaint Stone.

Named after Five Saints
The Pumsaint Stone is 3 feet tall and said to be named after five saints, whose names were Gwyn, Gwynno, Gwynoro, Ceitho and Cynfelyn. There are hollows in its four faces in which the saints are alleged to have left their footprints. The hollows are more likely to have been made by hand-held hammers crushing ore extracted from the adjoining gold mines at Dolaucothi which were worked for centuries, especially during Roman times, after their conquest of Wales in 75 AD. It was the only known Roman gold mine in Britain and the largest in the Roman Empire.

Location: Near the Dolaucothi Goldmines, situated off the A482 Llanwrda to Lampeter road. The site is now a National Trust visitor centre, Carmarthenshire – SN 656407 (146)

Megaliths of Wales: Mysterious Sites in the Landscape

Once Part of a 'One-Night House'

Maen Dewi standing stone was recorded as 'disappearing' one night when a local man took advantage of its enormous size, and, under the cover of darkness, hurriedly built against it a Hafod-un-Nos (one-night house). This was a technique often practiced in olden days for the claiming of common land for habitable dwellings. The house built the stone has vanished for the menhir now stands on its own.

Location: Dowrog Common, 2½ miles south-east of St David's, Pembrokeshire – SM 775275 (157)

Maen Dewi.

Standing Stones

Carreg Maen Taro.

Converted into a Boundary Stone

Carreg Maen Taro is a roughly hewn stone, which according to local tradition is said to mark the site of an ancient battle, but it is most likely a prehistoric standing stone. It is about 5 feet tall and has been used as a boundary stone with the letters 'B' and 'M' carved on two of its faces which indicate that it stands on the boundary between Brecknockshire and Monmouthshire.

Location: On the mountain ridge above Pwll-du, Monmouthshire – SO 238113 (161)

Gilestone.

An impressive stone
Gilestone is nearly 10 feet tall, 7 feet wide at the base and tapers to 3 feet at the top. It is one of several standing stones that can be found in the Usk Valley between Glangrwyney and Brecon.

Location: On private land at Gilestone Farm, to the north-east of Talybont-on-Usk, Brecknockshire – SO 117237 (161). Permission to visit this stone should be sought from the owners of the farm.

Standing Stones

A Stone Carried by the Devil

Garreg y Big (or Llech Bron) is 14 feet high and 9 feet in diameter at its base. It has a pointed top and in the mist it can look like a gigantic figure wrapped in a grey cloak: a strange sight which could well scare any nervous person seeing it for the first time by moonlight. One local story claims that the stone was carried from the top of Trichrug Mountain by the Devil when he was building his famous bridge across the Afon Mynach (popularly known as the Devil's Bridge). The stone was very heavy, so he sat down to rest for a while, until he was startled by the sudden crowing of a cock. He jumped up and fled, leaving the stone behind. If you look carefully and use your imagination you may see his fingerprints on the stone.

Location: Near Rhos Haminiog, Pembrokeshire – SN 542648 (146)

Garreg y Big.

Megaliths of Wales: Mysterious Sites in the Landscape

Harold Stone on Skomer Island.

An Island Standing Stone
Known as Harold Stone, this menhir can be seen on Skomer Island. It is about 5 feet high and tapers from a broad base to a point. Although it is not marked on the Ordnance Survey map, it is most probably a Bronze Age standing stone because it stands close to a prehistoric settlement consisting of huts and cairns.

Location: Near North Haven, Skomer Island, Pembrokeshire SM 733095 (157)

Standing Stones

Crossfoot Stone.

A Solitary Stone

Crossfoot standing stone, which is just under 5 feet high, was visited in 1870 by the Reverend Francis Kilvert, who wrote the following in his diary:

> I suppose that no one will ever know what the grey silent mysterious witness means, or why it was sent there. Perhaps it could tell some strange wild tales and many generations have flowed and ebbed it. There is something very solemn about these great solitary stones which stand about the country, monuments of some thing, but the memory has perished and the history forgotten.

Location: In a field near Crossfoot Farm, adjoining the minor road heading NNE from Clyro, Radnorshire – SO 219456 (148)

The Warrior Stone.

It Resembles the Head of a Greek Warrior
The Warrior Stone is a strange pillar-like stone of greyish-white rock over 6 feet high. It stands on top of a rock outcrop a few feet above the brow of a hill, which is partly covered over with earth and stones. From the east the outline of the Warrior Stone resembles a Greek warrior's head wearing a tall helmet, which explains why it is so-named.

Location: Bwlch Ungwr between Carngwr and Carn Breseb, Preseli Mountains, Pembrokeshire – SN 138330 (145)

2

Stone Rows

It is only to be expected that these great megalithic monuments of a prehistoric age should excite the wonder and stimulate the imagination of those who see them.

T. E. Peet, 1912

Stone alignments are quite rare in Wales, but one of the most interesting examples is a stone avenue which can be seen one mile above Pistyll Rhaeadr waterfall in the Tanat Valley. It is a double line of stones about 2 feet high, 10 feet apart and 190 feet long.

The longest existing stone row in Britain is on Stall Moor near Ivybridge on southern Dartmoor. It runs from a small stone circle on Green Hill for 2¼ miles. To see the most amazing prehistoric stone alignments in the world, one should go to Carnac, a World Heritage Site in Brittany, where there are unique alignments at Menec, Kermario and Erdeven. Within a distance of some 3,250 yards there are 2,813 menhirs, clearly orientated in an east-west direction, with no less than eleven parallel lines of stones, some over a mile long.

French water diviners have claimed that these stone rows mark eleven parallel underground streams. The stones are placed at 15-foot intervals with 30 feet between the rows and three hundred of them are more than 15 feet high. Many of the stones are missing, having been broken up through the centuries for use as building materials.

The three stones at Trellech.

The Trellech Stones

These three impressive stones are situated in a field near the village of Trellech and, standing in a straight line about 20 yards long, they point to the sky at a crazy angle. Sometimes they are referred to as Harold's Stones, because it was once claimed that they were erected to glorify his victory over the Britons and that they mark the burial place of some of his soldiers killed in battle. King Harold, the last of the Saxon kings, was killed at Hastings in 1066 and the stones were of course erected here in prehistoric times. They are composed of pudding-stone, which is best described as small pebbles enclosed in a hard cement-like material. Two cup marks can be seen on the south side of the central stone.

An alternative local explanation for the existence of these stones concerns a character called Jack o' Kent, who is said to have had a competition with the Devil and hurled these stones one after the other from the summit of Ysgyryd Fawr, about 12 miles away, near Abergavenny. They landed in this field on the outskirts of the village, which became known as Trellech (tri = three, llech = flat stone).

The stones are depicted on the base of a sundial, now to be seen in the village church. The numbers 7, 10 and 14 on the carvings of the stones are intended to refer to their heights, but they are in fact 9 feet, 12 feet and 15 feet tall.

Location: In a field just outside the village of Trellech, close to the Monmouth–Chepstow road, Monmouthshire – SO 498052 (162)

Stone Rows

This illustration of the Trellech Stones is from William Coxe's *Historic Tour in Monmouthshire* (1801). The man depicted makes the stones appears to be over 40 feet high!

Depiction of the three stones on the base of a font in the local church.

Megaliths of Wales: Mysterious Sites in the Landscape

The Gwytherin alignment.

The inscribed stone.

An Alignment of Four Stones

Gwytherin Church stands in a circular churchyard, which is an indication of a pagan site. Here can be seen a prehistoric alignment of four stones, each about 3 feet high and spaced at regular intervals of about 6 feet. One of the stones is inscribed with a fifth-century Latin inscription:

VINNEMAGLI FILI SENEMAGLI
(The Stone of Vinnemaglus son of Senemaglus)

The church was no doubt founded beside the stones in order to 'Christianise' the site.

Location: Gwytherin churchyard, on the B5384, Denbighshire – SH 876615 (116)

Stone Rows

The Pant Serthfa alignment.

An Alignment of Five Stones

The Pant Serthfa Row consists of five stones, but the largest has fallen. There is a single stone about 100 yards to the west of the row which is aligned north to south.

Location: On the south scarp of the Dyffryn Crawnon Valley in Brecknockshire – SO 118167 (161)

Megaliths of Wales: Mysterious Sites in the Landscape

An Alignment of Seven Stones

Saith Maen is situated at an altitude of 1,280 feet above sea level, on the slopes of Cribarth (Crest of the Bear), overlooking Craig y Nos Castle in the Swansea Valley, about ¾ mile above the A4067. On a level rock-strewn plateau is a line of stones about 10 yards long, running east to west. Five stones remain standing and are between 2 feet 6 inches and 5 feet in height. The two fallen stones are 9½ feet and 7½ feet long. Stones one to four and six to seven are of Millstone Grit, while stone five is of Old Red Sandstone The alignment points towards the stone circle of Cerrig Duon in the west and to another Saith Maen site across the valley to the east. It has been suggested that the row represents the Pleiades star group, the red stone representing the red star Merope.

According to local folklore the stones come alive on Midsummer night and roam the locality till sunrise. Anyone who saw them would die within a short time.

It is interesting that seven is the number of things sacred and mysterious such as the seven veils of initiation. According to Philo, 'nature delights in the number seven': the astrologers know seven planets, there are seven stars in the Great Bear constellation, seven colours of the rainbow, etc.

Location: On the slopes of Cribarth, about ¾ mile above the A4067 in the Swansea Valley, Brecknockshire – SN 833155 (160)

Saith Maen alignment.

Stone Rows

Saith Maen (East) alignment of boulders.

An Alignment of Seven Boulders

The Ordnance Survey map also names a Saith Maen on the slopes of Y Wern at an altitude of 1,400 feet. It is on the opposite side of the Swansea Valley to the line of standing stones called Saith Maen, and consists of a straight line of large erratic boulders which stand on a glaciated gritstone pavement. There are nine boulders in total and seven of them have been given the name Saith Maen (East). It is hard to know for certain if this indeed is a prehistoric alignment, but they do appear to have been deliberately placed in a straight line.

Location: Within the Ogof Ffynnon Ddu National Nature Reserve, south-east of Penwyllt, on the southern side of Carreg Lwyd, above the Swansea Valley, Brecknockshire – SN 862146 (160).

A similar alignment of boulders, known as Carreg Cadno (Fox Rock), has been identified not far away at SN 876156). This one consists of two stone rows at right-angles to each another and one stone forms the central point of each row. It is also of interest that one of the rows points in the same direction as Saith Maen (East).

Parc y Meirw alignment.

The Longest Megalithic Alignment in Wales

Parc y Meirw (Field of the Dead) is an impressive row of eight standing stones erected along a field boundary bank, over a distance of 160 feet in a NW/SE direction. Unfortunately, only four of the stones are still standing and one of them is 11 feet tall. There is a local tale of 'Ladi Wen' – a ghostly white lady who walks these fields at night and will kill anyone who comes near the stone row.

Another tradition maintains that the bodies of those killed in the eleventh-century battle of Mynydd Carn, which took place on the western slopes of the Preseli Hills, were buried here in a mass grave.

> *Four of the eight stones in this unusual row are trapped in a field wall, two of them now gateposts. [Professor]Thom suggested that the line, 131ft (40m) long, was laid downhill towards the WNW and the minor northern moon set just north of Mount Leinster ninety-one miles away across the Irish Sea.*
>
> Aubrey Burl

Location: Beside the B4313 Fishguard road ½ mile to the west of Trellwyn hamlet and 2 miles east of Llanychaer village, Pembrokeshire – SM 998359 (157)

3

Stone Circles

Stone Circles, along with other megalithic monuments of a prehistoric age should excite, wonder and stimulate the imagination of those who see them.

Ian Cooke

There are over 900 stone circles of varying sizes still in existence in the British Isles, dating from about 3300 BC to 1500 BC. They are to be found mostly in the upland areas and range in shape from true circles to ellipses, egg-shapes and flattened circles. In Wales the circles are not as impressive in size like those at Stonehenge or Avebury in England, but consist of small compact stones, usually about 3 to 4 feet in height.

The number of stones in a stone circle can vary from 4 to about 30, but one must take into account the fact that many of the smaller stones have been removed during the thousands of years that have passed since the stones were originally placed in a circle.

The stone circle with the largest individual erect stones in Wales is the Druid's Circle or Meini Hirion near Cefn Goch in the Parish of Dwygyfylch in Gwynedd (SH 722746). The tallest stone in this circle is 9 feet high.

Avebury in Wiltshire, with a diameter of 370 yards, is the largest stone circle in the British Isles. The largest stones weighed more than 40 tons and before many of them were broken up between the fourteenth and eighteenth centuries there was a total of 170 stones, but now only forty-three remain.

Over the passing centuries, a large number of stone circles have been destroyed through agricultural activities and road-building.

Gors Fawr Stone Circle.

One of the Best-Preserved Stone Circles in Wales

Gors Fawr Stone Circle is situated on rough moorland near Mynachlog-ddu, about 100 yards west of the main road at Llan. It is 70 feet in diameter and consists of sixteen glacial boulders set about 8 to 17 feet apart. It is not a true geometrical circle and the tallest stone is only 4 feet 4 inches in height. There are two prominent standing stones at the gap or entrance on the east side of the stone circle and about 10 yards further out on the east side is another large stone embedded in the earth which may have been placed in position by the stone-circle builders.

About 40 yards from the west side of the stone circle is a long, large maenhir lying prostrate which would have been about 6 feet high if it had been placed upright in the ground, and it would have been higher than any of the stones now forming part of the stone circle.

About 150 yards north-east of the stone circle are two larger erect greyish-green monoliths about 7 feet high and 15 yards apart. These do not stand out against the background to the north of the stone circle due to the high gorse, the buildings and the high stone walls of nearby Duffryn Dwndwr Farm. This name is of interest for while Duffryn means valley, the word Dwndwr means Hurlers, which is the name given for one of Cornwall's largest and best-known stone circles in the Parish of St Clear.

Stone Circles

Two stones to the east of Gors Fawr Circle.

Remains of an Embanked Stone Circle

Meini Gwyn (White Stones) is situated near Glandy Cross and the junction of five roads. This circle originally contained seventeen stones but now only two remain. This is the only circle in Pembrokeshire in which the stones are set upon a slightly embanked ring.

Professor Grimes excavated here in 1938 and found some Middle Bronze Age pottery. He measured the diameter of the circle and found it to be 60 feet; the outer bank was 100 feet in diameter and 3 feet high. There is a stone avenue 6 feet wide to the west of the circle. It originally had seventeen stones but only two now remain.

Meini Gwyn Circle.

Location: Near the village of Llandysillio East, beside the road to Maenclochog, Pembrokeshire – SN 142266 (145)

The Finest Stone Circle in North Wales

Y Meini Hirion (The Druid's Circle) stands on a grassy saddle on the Cefn Coch ridge at an altitude of 1,300 feet above sea level, at the junction of two trackways. This circle has a diameter of 80 feet, but only ten of the original thirty stones have survived and they are all nearly 6 feet in height. The central area was originally paved with white quartz. Although damaged by quarrying, the eastern part of the circle is intact.

There are two special stones in this circle. One of them, called the Deity Stone, was once held in considerable awe. It resembles a hooded human figure, with its head looking into the centre of the circle. They say that if anyone uses bad language near this stone, it will bend its head and hit the offending person! Immediately opposite is the Stone of Sacrifice, on top of which is a cavity large enough to hold a small child. There was once a belief that if a child was placed in this cavity for a few minutes during the first year of its life it would always be lucky.

An excavation in the centre of the circle during the 1950s revealed a cist covered with a capstone. Beneath it were found the cremated remains of a child of about 11 years of age.

Location: On Penmaenmawr headland, Caernarfonshire SH 723746 (115)

Y Meini Hirion (the Druid's Circle).

Moel Ty Uchaf Circle.

A Nearly Complete Stone Circle
Moel Ty Uchaf Circle in the Berwyn Mountains, 1,375 feet above sea level, is an almost perfect stone circle containing forty-one stones which are about 1½ feet tall and are spaced close together except for two wide gaps. At the centre is a stone-lined cist grave.

Location: On a hill overlooking the Dee Valley, to the east of Llandrillo, Denbighshire – SJ 055371 (125)

Tyfos Farmhouse Circle.

Fourteen Boulder Stones
Tyfos Stone Circle is situated in front of Tyfos Farmhouse, on a gently sloping field overlooking the River Dee, and consists of fourteen large boulders lying lengthways on the ground to form a circle, a raised platform. Few householders can claim to have a prehistoric stone circle in their front garden!

Location: Near Llandrillo, 4½ miles SW of Corwen, Denbighshire – SJ 0283387 (125)

Megaliths of Wales: Mysterious Sites in the Landscape

Cerrig Duon Stone Circle.

An Egg-Shaped Stone Circle
Cerrig Duon Circle (Black Stones) is an oval circle of stones (one of ten such circles discovered in Britain). It is situated on marshy ground, near the source of the River Tawe, at an altitude of 1,270 feet, and the twenty-one remaining stones are 1 to 2 feet in height. The diameter of the egg-shaped circle is 59 feet and its long axis lines up with the Saeth Maen stone row (see page 40).

An avenue of small stones leading from the stream to the circle consists of two rows of small stones placed lengthways in the direction of the alignment. The western row is 140 feet long and contains nineteen stones. The eastern row is 110 feet long and contains eleven stones.

The large block of sandstone 6 feet high is known as Maen Mawr (Great Stone) and it stands 30 feet to the north of Coed Duon Circle. The two small stones in front of it are in direct alignment to the north.

Location: In the Tawe Valley, to the west of the mountain road leading from Tafarn-y-garreg to Trecastle, Brecknockshire – SN 852206 (160)

Note: One has to cross the River Tawe on stepping stones to reach the site. This can be difficult when the river is swollen and fast-flowing.

Stone Circles

The large circle at Y Pigwyn.

The small circle at Y Pigwyn.

Y Pigwn Stone Circles
Two stone circles are situated on Mynydd Bach near the site of a Roman fort. The larger one to the north-east has a diameter of 76 feet with twenty-eight stones of about 1 foot in height. The smaller circle has a diameter of 25 feet and the stones are large, but only four remain.

It is interesting that on their conquering march westwards across Wales, the Romans destroyed any Celtic groves that they found in order to break the power of the Druids, but they generally seem to have left the Neolithic stone circles well alone.

Location: On Mynydd Bach, 1 mile north of Usk Reservoir, Brecknockshire – SN 833311 (160)

Cerrig Gaerall Circle.

The Remains of Two Stone Circles

To the south of Llanbrynmair on Newydd Fynddog Hill are two stone circles about 500 feet apart. One is called Cerrig Gaerall and is 69 feet in diameter with just eight stones still standing. The other circle is called Lled Craenhr Ych (the width of the skin of the ox). Its diameter is about 80 feet and there are only five stones remaining (about 2 feet high). It has been estimated that there were once fifteen stones in this circle. A solitary stone can be seen 100 feet outside the circle.

There is a legend that two ychain bannog (long-horned oxen) were separated by the Twymyn Valley. They stood on top of their respective hills and bellowed until they died of grief because they could not come together. The one that died on Newydd Fynddog was skinned and his skin marked by the circle of stones spread over the place of internment.

Location: Near Llanbrynmair, Montgomeryshire – SH 904005 (136)

Stone Circles

Gray Hill Stone Circle.

The Only Stone Circle in Monmouthshire
A stone circle can be found on the Mynydd Llwyd (Grey Hill) at an altitude of about 900 feet. It is 32 feet in diameter and may have once surrounded a large cairn of stones. In 1889 it was described as consisting of thirteen stones surrounding a cairn, the two prostrate stones being the remains of a burial chamber or cist. In summer the circle can be hidden by the bracken but the two outlying standing stones (6 feet and 7 feet tall) to the north-east can usually be seen.

In 1944 the Monmouthshire historian Fred Hando commented in *The Pleasant Land of Gwent*:

> *The two outer stones are in line with the midwinter sunrise point; the north-east stone and the inner stone (when raised) would be in line with the midwinter sunset point. My theory is that when the ancient observers saw their stones in line with these horizon sunrises and sunsets they were able to advise their agricultural tribesmen that the seasons were changing. Such knowledge was power!*

Location: 4 miles north-west of Caerwent on the south-eastern side of Mynydd Llwyd (Gray Hill), Monmouthshire – ST 437935 (171)

Megaliths of Wales: Mysterious Sites in the Landscape

Carn Lechart.

Remains of the central rectangular cist.

An Impressive Cairn Circle

Carn Lechart is one of the largest ring cairns in Britain. It is similar in appearance to Bryn Cader Faner stone circle (see page 53) and consists of seventeen slabs of stone set in a circle 95 feet in diameter and leaning slightly outwards. They stand out against the skyline like a coronet and surround a central rectangular cist of which the east side and the capstone are missing.

This monument was first mentioned by William Camden in 1695. In his book *Britannia* he describes it as 'a circle of rude stones which are somewhat of a flat form.'

Location: On top of Carn Lechart Mountain, NW of Pontardawe in the upper Swansea Valley, Glamorgan – SN 697063 (159)

Stone Circles

Bryn Cader Faner Stone Circle.

The Crown of Thorns

Bryn Cader Faner is an unusual Bronze Age monument which is a combination of a stone circle and a burial mound. It has been described by Professor Aubrey Burl as one of the 'wonders of prehistoric Wales'. It consists of fifteen stones remaining of the original thirty. Each one is about 6 feet high and leans outwards to give the appearance of a crown of thorns and is particularly impressive when photographed silhouetted against the sky. The large cist in the centre once contained human remains.

Treasure hunters dug into the cairn centre in the nineteenth century and the hole they made is still visible. During the Second World War the army used the cairn for target practice.

Location: Llandecwyn, 5 miles NE of Harlech, Merionethshire – SH 648353 (124). To reach the site one has to undertake a 4-mile walk, involving careful navigation over difficult ground.

> *You have to settle for the fact that there are large areas of the past that we cannot find out about. Stone circles are barren archaeological sites. There is almost nothing in them to suggest what went on there, and absolutely nothing has ever been found which has enabled us to know with certainty what they were for.*
>
> Professor Richard Atkinson

Carn Menyn, where the bluestones of Stonehenge were quarried.

Source of the Stonehenge Bluestones
Carn Menyn (Cairn of the Boulders), an outcrop on Mynydd Preseli, is believed to be the main source of the bluestones of Stonehenge. A half-finished bluestone even lies there (GR 142325). It has been hammered along two faces and has a 'club foot'. Carnalw, 1 mile to the north, provided four rhydolite stones.

Preseli Bluestone or Spotted Dolerite is an igneous rock which was used for the manufacture of polished stone tools such as axes. The dark blue-black grained texture is speckled with white spots of feldspar, and it is called bluestones because of their colour in wet weather.

It was Dr H.H. Thomas of the Geological Survey who, in 1923, put forward the idea that the thirty bluestones of Stonehenge originated from the Preseli Mountains. He stated:

> The assemblage of Stonehenge's foreign stones presents the significant feature of derivation from a comparatively small area where all the various rock types occur together. Such an area may be limited by the actual outcrops of rock in question or the stones may have been taken from the boulder-strewn slopes in the immediate south and south-east of the Preseli between Carnmeini and Cilmaen Llwyd where all their types have been collected together by glacial action.

He later added:

> It is probably more than a coincidence that this area, clearly indicated by geological evidence as the source of the Stonehenge foreign stones, should contain one of the richest collections of megalithic remains in Britain.

Stone Circles

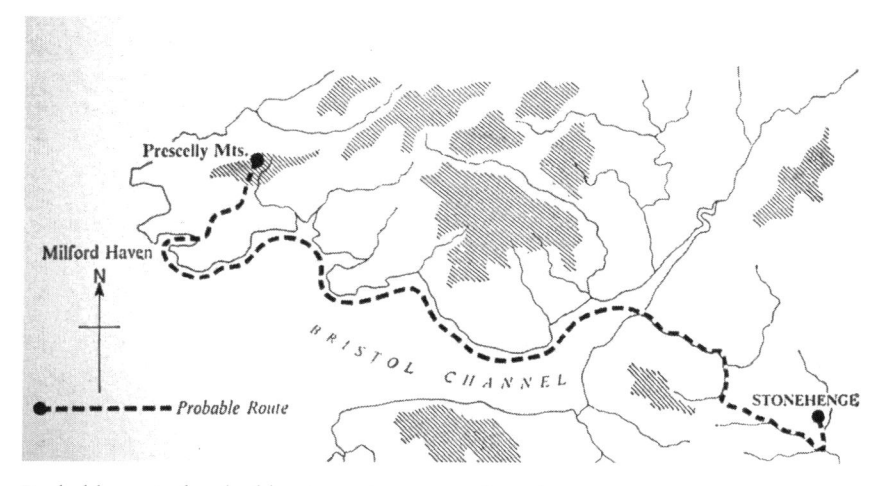

Probable route for the bluestones journey to Stonehenge.

Professor R.J. Atkinson, author of *Stonehenge*, considers that at least ninety bluestones, each weighing about 4 and 7 tons, were taken from the Carnalw and Carnmenyn to Salisbury Plain in Wiltshire to erect the sacred heart of Stonehenge.

The Bluestone Circle, now much ruined and incomplete, stands inside the Sarsen Circle. Originally it consisted of about sixty stones, set close together. It was probably the work of the Beaker people, who colonised Britain from the Continent at the end of the Neolithic period.

The bluestones were probably brought to Stonehenge mainly by water, loaded on rafts or boats. The most likely route runs from Milford Haven, along the south coast of Wales and up the Bristol Channel to Avonmouth; then up the Avon and Frome rivers to near Frome in Somerset, overland to near Warminster, and from there by the Wylye and the Salisbury Avon to the end of the Stonehenge Avenue, a total distance about 240 miles (385km).

Such a journey was in fact proved possible by a party of schoolboys in 1954, using rafts. They had to travel just 25 miles across land.

The altar stone which is 16 feet long also came from Pembrokeshire. It is composed of pale green micaceous sandstone and is believed to have come from the Cosheston beds on the shores of Milford Haven.

In 1988 a bluestone block was discovered on the bed of the River Daugleddau at Llangwm in Pembrokeshire. It is of similar size to those used at Stonehenge and probably accidently fell into the sea whilst being loaded onto a raft.

Megaliths of Wales: Mysterious Sites in the Landscape

It is of interest that in 1140 Geoffrey of Monmouth, claimed that Merlin took down the 'Giant's Round', a circle of standing stones on 'Mount Killaraus in Ireland' and erected them in their present position at Stonehenge on the downs in Wiltshire. For nearly 800 years this was considered one of Geoffrey's most incredible stories. Then in 1923 Dr Herbert Thomas, a petrogapher to the British Geological Survey, showed that the inner standing stones of Stonehenge originated in the Preseli Hills in Pembrokeshire, Wales. It is possible that this was a transference of what was already a sacred monument and Geoffrey's strange statement stemmed from an oral tradition relating to the erection of the bluestones 2,500 years previously.

It is relevant that in the Dark Ages the area of the Preseli Hills was colonised by the Irish. They were ruled by an Irish king and Goedelic was the spoken language. So this locality was just like a small part of Ireland in the reputed time of Merlin, which could well explain the reason for Geoffrey of Monmouth's statement. The bluestones can only be found in an area of one square mile between the outcrops of Carn Meini and Foel Trigarn at the eastern end of the Preseli Hills.

An actual stone circle was removed from the eastern end of the Preseli ridge and taken to Salisbury Plain. The foreign stones remaining within Stonehenge are thirty-four in number – twenty-nine dolerite (bluestones) four rhyolite boulders and one sandstone. It is significant that the four rhyolite boulders are identical in colour and mineralogical details with the rhyolite boulders found on Carnaliw in the Preseli range.

The probability that the Preseli Mountains may have been an area of special holiness at the time of the Stone Age or beginning of the Bronze Age is suggested by the presence there of several small circles which doubtless indicate the former existence of a considerably large number.

This tremendous feat of prehistoric transport implies some very exceptional religious motive and the transfer of the stones suggests the complete or partial transference of a particularly sacred centre from an older home in Pembrokeshire to a newer home in Wiltshire.

Sir Mortimer Wheeler

Location: North of Mynachlog-ddu, Preseli Mountains, Pembrokeshire – SN 140320 (145)

4
Cromlechs and Dolmens

To the lovers of cromlechs and dolmens, Anglesey is a treasure island and they turn to it with joy.

A.G. Bradley

Cromlech and dolmen are terms that are both used to describe a stone tomb that has no earth-covering mound, the massive capstone and supporting stones being exposed. The word cromlech is Welsh for 'bent flagstone' and was first used to describe a prehistoric tomb by the sixteenth-century Pembrokeshire historian, George Owen. The word dolmen was invented by the French archaeologist Canet in 1796, being derived from the Breton words *tol* (table) and *men* (stone). It describes structures which are in the form of a prehistoric stone table consisting of standing stones balancing one or more flat capstones on top, forming a kind of primitive chamber. The number of supporting stones under the capstone vary, but they do not seem to number more than ten. From now on I will use the word Cromlech as I am referring to megaliths in Wales (the plural being cromlechau).

The weight of the capstones of the larger cromlechs is often over 25 tons and such massive stones would need very careful handling to place them so precisely on top of a number of upright stones. Such labour would have involved the co-operation of many hands and we can assume therefore that these people were socially organised in small clans or large family groups living in settled communities.

These constructions can be seen as stone wombs into which the dead were placed for rebirth. A forecourt outside the chamber was provided for ceremonies to be held while the recently dead person was placed within, accompanied by their grave goods, for use on their long journey to another world.

Like our own family vaults, the burial chambers might be used again and again for successive generations. Occasionally they have been found to contain large numbers of skeletons and with clear signs that the old corpses have been pushed aside to make room for new ones.

Within the British Isles there are about 2,000 megalithic tombs and these include about 1,000 in Ireland, 350 in Scotland, about 250 in England and about 400 in Wales. These structures were erected during the period 2000 BC to 1500 BC and have also been found in Malta, Sicily, Spain, Southern France, Brittany, and as far east as India and Japan.

Some were built with entrance passages and were constructed in such a way that access was available for later additional burials. These tombs were apparently built as communal burial chambers for use over a long period. However, not every person in Neolithic Britain would have been entitled to burial inside a tomb. They were more likely reserved for the leaders of communities and their families.

Cromlechs are found in many parts of Wales but mostly within easy reach of the sea in the lower hills and valley sides. A number of people were often buried in the same tomb, probably over a period of many years. The skulls found in them are of a type which are long from back to front and belonged to people of short or medium height.

Anglesey is the finest area in Wales for studying burial chambers, for there are a greater number of Neolithic tombs to be seen on this island than in any other part of Wales. But of the numerous cromlechau that are known to have existed on Anglesey, only twenty-five now remain, and of this number just nine can be said to be in a good state of preservation. The others have shed their capstones, or their supports have collapsed, and in two instances only fragments of the stones remain. Thirteen of the recorded sites have even disappeared completely, leaving no trace whatsoever.

There has been a great deal of discussion as to whether the cromlechs were originally covered with a tumulus which has been removed by erosion, but the following arguments suggest that this is unlikely:

1. The similarity of these megalithic chambers makes it highly probable that they were all constructed for one and the same purpose.
2. Huge numbers of these monuments can be seen with no trace of a former covering mound.
3. Some of the chambers have holed stones that were surely not intended to be covered up, for the holes, whatever their purpose, would then be of no use.

Cromlechs and Dolmens

4. It is possible that these structures were intended to be seen and were constructed as 'mortuary chapels' with their sides filled in with stones.
5. It seems hard to believe that these structures, which had involved so much labour, should have been intended by the builders to be concealed within a mound. It seems incredible that people should go to the trouble of raising huge capstones and placing them on the points of supporting stones with such precision and then hide them from view.

The Finest Cromlech in Monmouthshire

Gaer Llwyd, also known as Garn Lwyd (grey Fortress), can be found in a field near crossroads on the B4235 Usk to Chepstow road at an altitude of 700 feet. Five of the supporting stones remain, although the one at the north end has fallen inwards. They vary in height from 3 feet to 4½ feet and are composed of conglomerate. Their arrangement would suggest that the burial chamber was a double one or that a supplementary cist was added at one end. The covering stone must have been very large before it was broken and it still measures 12 feet by 5 feet and is 9 to 12 inches thick.

Location: In a field near crossroads on the B4235, between Usk and Shirenewton, Monmouthshire – ST 447968 (171)

Gaer Llwyd Cromlech.

Megaliths of Wales: Mysterious Sites in the Landscape

Gwern y Cleppa Cromlech.

Another Monmouthshire Cromlech

Gwern y Cleppa Cromlech, just to the west of Newport, was once a structure of considerable size. Three upright stones in situ, but one of the supports, more than 4 feet in length, lies under the capstone. A portion of this covering slab which lies embedded in the ground is composed of Siliceous sandstone. Originally the structure probably occupied an area about 12 feet square. The cist lay south-east and north-west with a covering mound about 50 feet in diameter. According to old records an oak tree once overshadowed the stones.

Location: In a field adjoining Maes Arthur and to the north of the M4 near Tredegar Park, outside Newport, Monmouthshire – ST 272860 (171)

Cromlechs and Dolmens

Ystumcegid Cromlech.

A Very Long Capstone

Ystumcegid Cromlech is also known as Coetan Arthur and Arthur's Quoit, because it is said to have been thrown there by Arthur from a hill near Beddgelert. It is very impressive with a capstone 15 feet long. Originally it was a triple cromlech but by 1816 there was only one chamber remaining, which was used as a sheepfold, and described as high enough for a man on horseback to ride into.

Location: On farmland near Dinas Cross, 2 miles north of Criccieth in the Parish of Llanfihangel y Pennant, Caernarfonshire – SH 498413 (123)

Hendre Waelod Cromlech.

Another Mighty Capstone
Hendre Waelod Cromlech, also known as Allor Molach (Molach's Altar), is situated in a field near Glan Conwy. It has a 22-ton capstone which is one of the heaviest in Wales and is 3 feet thick. It has unfortunately slipped out of position.

Location: On the eastern side of the Conwy Valley on the lower slopes of Bryniau, Denbighshire – SH 793747 (115)

Cromlechs and Dolmens

Tinkinswood Cromlech near Cardiff.

The Largest Capstone in Britain

Tinkinswood Cromlech is named after a nearby farm but it also known as Llech y Filiast and Castell Carreg. In Brittany, carreg or carrigan means fairy, and it was once thought that fairies lived in cromlechau. The group of boulders to the south of this monument are said to be women turned to stone for dancing on a Sunday.

The single massive capstone is 28 feet long by 18 feet wide, about 2 feet thick and weighs over 40 tons. It is now cracked and has slipped out of position. The chamber underneath measures 18 feet by 15 feet and is about 5½ feet high. All the stones in this monument are made of a Triassic mudstone, quarried from a thin layer which outcrops locally.

This monument was excavated in 1914 by John Ward and finds belonging to three distinct cultures were identified. Roman pottery and objects of iron indicated that it was opened during this period. Fragments of bones found, included the remains of some fifty individuals consisting of eight children, twenty-one females and sixteen males. Neolithic flints and animal bones were found near the forecourt entrance and Beaker-style pottery indicated that the tomb was still in use during the early Bronze Age. The herringbone walling on the right at the entrance to the burial chamber is modern.

Location: Situated in a field at Tinkinswood, near St Nicholas, Glamorgan – ST 082733 (171)

Megaliths of Wales: Mysterious Sites in the Landscape

The Spinning Capstone

St Lythan's Cromlech is a very impressive monument which is also known as Gwal-y-Filiast (the Greyhound Bitch's Lair), and this name may come from an Arthurian tale in the *Mabinogion*. It consists of three upright stones and a triangular capstone enclosing a chamber 7 feet 6 inches by 6 feet and 6 feet high. It is rectangular in plan and open at the south end. The side stones are about 12 feet long by 7 feet 6 inches broad and the end stone measures 5 feet by 6 feet. There is a hole in this stone through which it was probably once believed that the spirit of the dead would take flight. The capstone measures 14 feet by 10 feet and all the stones are about 2 feet thick. The structure was once covered with a mound about 90 feet long and as at nearby Tinkinswood the single capstone, like the uprights, is of local Triassic mudstone.

On Midsummer Eve the capstone is supposed to spin three times, and if you make a wish there on Halloween it will come true. The field in which this cromlech stands is known as the 'Accursed Field' and it is claimed that nothing will grow there.

Location: At Duffryn in a field (called Maesfelin – 'The Mill Field') near a road junction about half a mile south-east of Duffryn House, Glamorgan – ST 100722 (171)

St Lythan's Cromlech.

Lligwy Cromlech.

A Very Thick Capstone
Lligwy Cromlech has a massive capstone which weighs about 28 tons and measures 18 feet by 16 feet and is 3½ feet thick. It is supported on a number of small uprights which hold it about 6 feet above the base of an irregular pit. It was excavated in 1909.

This ancient monument is also called Arthur's Quoit (Coetan Arthur) and it was once believed to be the site of a hoard of treasure. A story is told how a farm steward was heard to remark that he intended to dig for the gold one night and one of his friends decided to play a trick on him. He dug a hole in the ground near the cromlech and pressed the bottom of a pot into the hole and then removed it in order to give the impression that someone had been there and found a pot of gold. Draped in a white sheet he took up a position a short distance away and waited. In due course the treasure seeker arrived and was dumbfounded when he saw the impression of the pot; but this was nothing to what was in store for him. Looking up, he was terrified to see a ghostly white figure rise from the ground. The treasure seeker threw down his lamp and tools and ran home as fast as his legs would carry him, to the great satisfaction of the 'ghost'!

Location: SW of Moelfre on the A5205 on the side of the road leading to Chapel Lligwy, Anglesey – SH 501861 (114)

Carreg Coetan Arthur.

One of Arthur's Quoits
Carreg Coetan Arthur is also known as Arthur's Quoit and it can be found near a small housing estate on the east side of Newport in Pembrokeshire. A massive wedge-shaped capstone is supported by only two of the four original sidestones. It was excavated in 1979 and 1980 and is believed to date from 3,500 BC. The 'coetan' part of the name refers to the old game of quoits which is often associated with burial chambers and in this instance suggests that King Arthur played the game using the capstone.

Location: In a small field at Newport, Pembrokeshire – SN 063391 (145)

Cromlechs and Dolmens

Another Coetan Arthur at St David's Head.

One of Many Cromlechs Associated with King Arthur
Coetan Arthur stands on open moorland above the cliffs of St David's Head. A large capstone is supported on one side by a side stone about 4 feet high. Two other sidestones lie prostrate beneath the capstone.

Location: St David's headland, Pembrokeshire – SM 725280 (157)

King's Quoit Cromlech.

A Burial Chamber in a Dramatic Situation
King's Quoit is perched on the edge of a cliff overlooking Manorbier Bay. The large capstone is 15 feet long by 9 feet wide and 12 inches thick. It is supported at one end by two short pillars while the other end rests on the ground. There are fine views from here across the bay.

Location: On the side of the coastal path at Old Castle Head above Manorbier Bay, Pembrokeshire – SS 059973 (158)

Cromlechs and Dolmens

The two Dyffryn Ardudwy Cromlechs.

The Dyffryn Ardudwy Cromlechs

Two impressive cromlechs have been exposed by the removal of a massive covering cairn that would have originally been about 130 feet long and 55 feet wide. The two burial chambers are about 25 feet apart, and the largest one has a capstone measuring about 10 feet square and nearly 2 feet thick. They are variously referred to as Arthur's Quoit, Carreg Arthur or Coetan Arthur.

Location: Dyffryn Ardudwy, off the A496, about 7 miles north of Barmouth, Gwynedd – SH 588228 (124)

Maen y Bardd.

Kennel of the Greyhound
Maen y Bardd (stone of the Bard) is also known as Cwrt y Filiast, Llech yr Ast and Cwrt y Bugail. It is situated to the west of Rowen on the north side of the Roman road leading to Bwlch y Ddeufaen (see page…). The capstone which rests on four upright stones is 2½ feet thick and measures 12 feet 9 inches by 8 feet. The local name for it is Cwrt y Filiast (Kennel of the Greyhound). The structure was originally covered with a stone cairn, the remains of which can still be seen at the monument.

Location: On the southern slope of Tal y Fan Mountain, high above the Conwy Valley, Caernarfonshire – SC 741718 (115)

Cromlechs and Dolmens

Carreg Samson.

Named after St Samson

Samson's Quoit is known in Welsh as Carreg Samson and is also called the Longhouse Cromlech after a nearby farm. It is an impressive monument, 15 feet long and 9 feet broad and has six supports. The local legend is that St Samson lifted the capstone in place with his little finger, which he cut off in the process! This large stone is 6 feet above the ground and slopes down towards the sea. About 500 yards to the north-west is a small islet on which a mound is called 'The Grave of Samson's Finger'.

St Samson was born in the Vale of Glamorgan in about 490 AD and ended up as Bishop of Dol in Brittany, where he died in 565 AD. It is possible that he is associated with this monument because Samson is a corruption of the Welsh word simson, which means 'unsteady' or 'tottering' – an appropriate description for the capstone looks quite precarious!.

Location: Between Trevine and Abercastell at Ty Hir (Long House), Pembrokeshire – SM 848335 (157)

Bodwyr Cromlech.

A Very Distinctive Capstone
Bodwyr Cromlech has a large capstone which looks like a giant mushroom. It is 8 feet long and 6 feet wide and is supported by three upright stones. A fourth one lies prostrate on the ground.

Location: In a field, 1 mile east of Llangaffo, Anglesey – SH 462682 (114)

Cromlechs and Dolmens

Plas Newydd Cromlech.

An Impressive Cromlech

Plas Newydd Cromlech stands in the grounds of Plas Newydd Park, the one-time home of Lord Anglesey, situated beside the Menai Strait. It is now managed by the National Trust and visitors are only allowed to see this monument from the car park. It is one of the best-known cromlechs in Wales and is remarkable for the size of its chamber and coverstone. There are two adjacent chambers, one larger than the other, with massive uprights and capstones separated by a single upright.

Location: Off the A4080, about 1½ miles from Llanfair PG on the Plas Newydd Estate, Anglesey – SH 520697 (114)

Ty Newydd Cromlech.

Another Large Capstone
Ty Newydd Cromlech has a massive capstone, 13 feet by 5 feet, resting on three uprights. When it was excavated in 1938, no human bones were found, but finds included 110 pieces of white quartz in a layer of charcoal, beaker fragments, a barbed arrowhead and a flint chip which may have come from a polished axehead.

Location: On the crest of a broad ridge near the road at Ty Newydd, Anglesey – SH 344739 (114)

Cromlechs and Dolmens

Pentre Ifan Cromlech.

The Largest and Finest Cromlech in Wales
Pentre Ifan (Ivan's Village) is situated to the south-east of Newport on a foothill of Mynydd Preselli, overlooking the Nevern estuary. The route to it along lanes and a footpath is clearly signposted from the main road.

The massive capstone is 17 feet long by 9 feet across. It is balanced on the points of three tall uprights and is 7 feet 6 inches above the ground. It is high and wide enough for six people on horseback to shelter beneath it.

This amazing structure was excavated by Professor Grimes in 1936–7 and 1958–9, to be subsequently restored by the Ministry of Works, when it was in danger of collapsing. Originally it would have been covered by a cairn, estimated to be 130 feet long and 65 feet wide at the higher end where the entrance would have been. The limits of this mound are marked by small boulders.

There is a famous painting of Pentre Ifan by Richard Tonge of Bath in about 1830. He was well known as a 'painter and modeller of megaliths' and gave the impression that the capstone is virtually floating above the burial chamber by making the supporting stones taller and more slender than they actually are.

Location: Signposted off the A487, near Nevern, Pembrokeshire – SH 099370 (145)

Megaliths of Wales: Mysterious Sites in the Landscape

Pentre Ifan is high enough for people on horseback to shelter underneath it.

Pentre Ifan at sunset.

5

Gallery Graves, Long Cairns and Chambered Tombs

The burial places which are called barrows are to be seen all over the world. They can be found in North Africa, Siberia, China, and Japan, as well as Egypt, South America and throughout Europe.

Gilbert Stone

Gallery graves appear to have originated in western France in the region of the Loire and southern Brittany. The English and Welsh gallery graves were built by small groups of immigrants who sailed up the Bristol Channel and settled the coast on either side, landing on Gower and at the western end of the Cotswolds. They eventually colonised the Brecknockshire Black Mountains, the Gloucestershire Cotswolds and the eastern end of the Mendips.

A gallery grave consists of a rectangular chamber inside a long mound. It is a form of communal burial site for multiple burials, for it could be opened to receive new occupants. There would usually be additional small chambers leading off the gallery.

Long cairns, introduced in Neolithic times, are large mounds of earth, often about 100 to 300 feet long, 30 to 100 feet wide and between 4 and 12 feet high. The highest point is always at the wide end, and they are normally aligned east-west, facing the rising and setting sun.

Chambered tombs consist of a round cairn or mound with a long, narrow stone-lined passage leading from the outside to a polygonal symmetrical chamber. Two good examples in North Wales are Bryn Celli Ddu and Barclodiad y Gawres on Anglesey.

Megaliths of Wales: Mysterious Sites in the Landscape

Heston Brake Chambered Tomb is near the Severn Estuary.

The Most Easterly Chambered Tomb in Wales
Heston Brake, situated on the brow of a hill overlooking the Severn Estuary near Black Rock, is the easternmost of the Welsh chambered tombs. There were originally two chambers contained inside the covering mound (which has been ploughed away) with the entrance on the east side between two large blocks of stone. One of the stones is 6 feet high and the total length of the structure must have been about 70 feet. The two chambers are not in line but are placed end to end and are even of different levels, although they are intercommunicating. This seems to explain the suggestion that the western chamber (about 9 feet in length) was added to the eastern and earlier chamber, which is about 13 feet in length.

The site was excavated in 1888 and in the first chamber (which measures 13 feet by 5 feet) were found some ox bones, human teeth and finger bones. The smaller western room was also found to contain human bones and it has two upright stones with holes cut into them.

If you would like to feel shivers down your spine, choose a moonlit midnight next summer and visit this long barrow alone.
Fred J. Hando, 1954

Location: Near Portskewett, Monmouthshire – ST 506887 (171)

Gallery Graves, Long Cairns and Chambered Tombs

Capel Garmon Long Barrow.

A Classic Example of a Gallery Grave

Capel Garmon is a Neolithic long barrow sometimes called Yr Ogof (The Cave). It is shaped like a wedge with a horned forecourt at the east end, where there is a false entrance. The real entrance was on the south side via a passage leading to two burial chambers, laid out in the form of a figure 8. Only the western portion of the chamber has kept its large capstone, which is supported by eight upright stones.

It was built when the design of this type of tomb had been modified. The forecourt was no longer used to lead to the entrance, but was built as a dummy, and the entrance to the three-chambered gallery was made through a passage from the long side of the wedge-shaped cairn. A wall, straight sided, defined the cairn and forecourt, and over this, soon after the chamber and passages were built, a larger oblong mound was raised to conceal everything from view.

In 1925 pottery dating from 1800 BC was found in the entrance passage. Until the middle of the nineteenth century this monument appears to have been intact, but then one of the roofing slabs was removed and at one time the chamber was even used as a stable!

Location: Situated high above the Conwy Valley, 1 mile south of the village of Capel Garmon, Denbighshire – SH 818543 (116)

Bedd yr Afanc Gallery Grave.

A Gallery Grave with Transepts
Bedd yr Afanc (The Monster's Grave) is a gallery grave dating from 2,500 BC. It is unusual for this area that the burials were made in transepts leading off the main corridor. The chamber, which is built from quite small stones, is 30 feet long, wedge-shaped in plan, tapering from 6 feet to 3 feet, and set in the centre of a roughly rectangular mound. No capstones have survived.

Location: Situated in the middle of a moor, it is reached by a half-mile walk from Brynberiau Road, Pembrokeshire – SN 109346 (145)

Gallery Graves, Long Cairns and Chambered Tombs

Carneddau Hengwm Southern Long Cairn.

Two Remote Long Cairns

Carneddau Hengwm is situated about 900 feet above sea level and consists of a group of huge Neolithic burial mounds, aligned east-west and 50 yards apart. They are situated just south of Afon Egryn and are difficult to locate for there are so many stone walls that the stone cairns, although massive, are hard to see from a distance.

The northern cairn is about 100 feet long and 50 feet wide. Near the centre can be seen the remains of a circular stone wall about 9 feet in diameter. The capstone that once covered this chamber can be seen near the west end of the cairn and is about 12 feet by 10 feet.

The southern cairn is the most impressive and would originally have been about 200 feet long by 70 feet wide and 8 feet tall, but the western end has unfortunately been destroyed. Near the centre is a chamber covered by a large capstone. Access is by a narrow passage, about 3 feet wide, on the north side. The remnants of another chamber can be seen about 30 yards to the east of the middle chamber and it would appear that there were originally at least two other small side chambers as well.

Location: On a hillside above the A496, about 5 miles north of Barmouth, Merioneth – SH 613205 (124)

Gwernvale Long Cairn.

An Excavated Long Cairn

Gwernvale Long Cairn has been dated to 3,000 BC and was first excavated by Sir Richard Colt Hoare in 1808. The capstone that he prized off was evidently destroyed. Following the re-alignment of the A40 to the south of the site it was again excavated in the summer of 1978 by the Clwyd Powys Archaeological Trust. This excavation revealed eight upright slabs forming a polygonal chamber with a short approach passage.

This trapezodical (wedge-shaped) cairn was over 45 yards in length with a recessed forecourt at its eastern end. It was found to enclose three chambers with a possible fourth chamber or cist at its western end. The structure is orientated east/west and edged by an inner and outer drystone wall of which only the lower courses have survived. Unfortunately, the capstones of the chamber have at some time been removed.

The chambers within the cairn were no doubt used for communal burials by agricultural communities living in the vicinity. A substantial amount of Neolithic artifacts were found within the chambers, including polished flint implements, numerous arrowheads and a polished stone axe. The original area of the tomb is marked by small stones which have been set in the ground by the archaeologists.

Location: Just west of Crickhowell beside the A40, on the grass verge near the entrance drive to Gwernvale Manor Hotel, Brecknockshire – SO 211192 (161)

Gallery Graves, Long Cairns and Chambered Tombs

Bedd Taliesin Long Cairn.

Once Believed to Be the Grave of Taliesin
Bedd Taliesin is situated on a lonely hillside to the north-east of Talybont, on the slopes of Moel y Garn. It consists of a large stone slab and a cairn. The other stones have been removed over the years, probably by farmers looking for suitable stones for use as gateposts.

At one time this long cairn was claimed to be the grave of the bard Taliesin, who is mentioned in the *Mabinogion* and lived in the sixth century. A story is told how an attempt was made to find his bones in the nineteenth century, with the aim of moving them to a more holy site. But while the men were digging, they were suddenly startled by a violent thunderstorm. Lightning flashed and struck the ground with a loud crack. They fled for their lives, leaving their tools behind. They never returned to try again.

Location: Situated near Gwarcwm Uchaf on the side of the mountain above the Dovey Estuary, Cardiganshire – SN 672912 (124)

Megaliths of Wales: Mysterious Sites in the Landscape

Din Dryfal Chambered Tomb.

Remains of a Chambered Tomb
Din Dryfal Chambered Tomb has a gallery which is aligned from east to west. At the eastern end the entrance is about 6 feet wide and flanked by two large slabs. The total length of the gallery was about 48 feet. A huge portal stone at the east end marks the entrance to a series of four rectangular chambers. The whole structure was covered by a low cairn about 200 feet long.

Location: North of Bethel, with access by a footpath from a lane off the B4422, Anglesey – SH 395724 (114)

Gallery Graves, Long Cairns and Chambered Tombs

The Most Westerly Long Cairn in Wales

Parc le Breos Tomb is one of the most important archaeological finds in Wales. Known variously as The Giant's Grave, Parc le Breos Tomb or Parc Cwm Long Cairn, it is of the Cotswold/Severn type and the most westerly example in Wales. This well-preserved tomb was opened in 1869 by Sir John Lubbock who recorded that this communal burial place was occupied by:

> Men, women and children at all stages of life who had their remains mingled together; twenty four in all, including 3 children between 8 and 11 years old, 2 very old persons (over 70 years), the rest between 25 and 45 years.

It was Sir John Lubbock (later Lord Avebury) who introduced the word Neolithic (New Stone Age) into the English language. In 1882, this Liberal MP pushed the Ancient Monuments Bill through Parliament, having been appalled at the treatment of Britain's ancient monuments. They could be excavated by antiquarian enthusiasts or landowners at will with no attempts made to record their discoveries. The Bill was supported by the recently formed Society for the Protection of Ancient Buildings and, despite a certain amount of ridicule, it was duly passed.

In 1937 the site was re-excavated by Professor Glyn Daniel, who revealed it to be an elongated barrow and not a round one as first thought. The present condition of the tomb has resulted from the careful consolidation carried out by Professor Atkinson in 1961 on behalf of the Department of the Environment.

Location: In Green Cwm, north-west of Parkmill, Glamorgan – SS 537898 (159)

Parc le Breos Long Cairn.

The Best Assembly of Megalithic Art in Wales

Barclodiad y Gawres ('The Apronful of the Giantess') derives its name from a tradition shared with a number of sites in Britain, that they were formed by a giantess carrying an apronful of stones that she dropped when the strings on her apron snapped. It originally consisted of a cairn about 90 feet in diameter, constructed partly of rubble and partly of turves. At the centre is a megalithic chamber, cross-shaped in plan and approached from the north by a 23-feet-long passage. There are three smaller side chambers, each of which would have been covered with a capstone, but only the southern one has survived.

The excavators in 1952–3 found a strange mixture of burnt remains in the centre of the chamber, consisting of part of a pig's vertebra, whiting, eels, a frog, a toad, a snake, a mouse, a shrew and a hare. This strange assortment was described as a 'witch's brew'. After the twentieth-century excavation of the site was completed, a reinforced concrete dome was erected over the chamber to protect its decorated slabs, and the whole thing then covered with earth and turf. The original mound, remains of which can be seen, would have been about 90 feet in diameter.

Barclodiad y Gawres.

Gallery Graves, Long Cairns and Chambered Tombs

One of the decorated stones inside the chamber.

Five of the large stones that form the walls of the chamber are decorated with spiral and zig-zag patterns. These carvings are similar to those at Newgrange in Ireland, which has thirty visible decorated stones consisting mainly of complex lozenges and spirals. A torch is needed to examine the interior. It is kept locked to avoid damage by vandals and graffiti artists.

Location: Situated on a headland overlooking Trecastell Bay (Cable Bay), Rhosneigr, near Castle Bay, Aberffraw, signposted off the A4080, Anglesey – SH 329707 (114)

Megaliths of Wales: Mysterious Sites in the Landscape

The Finest Passage Grave in Wales

Bryn Celli Ddu (The Mound of the Dark Grave) has been raised within a circular henge. It is the finest example in England and Wales of a type of burial chamber well known in Ireland and Scotland in which a large polygonal chamber is approached along a narrow passage. The whole structure was then covered by a round cairn, or mound, 85 feet in diameter. The modern mound that one sees today only covers a small part of the area of the prehistoric mound, which was 160 feet in diameter. It was excavated in 1928.

Bryn Celli Ddu Passage Grave.

Bryn Celli Ddu as it appeared in 1847.

Gallery Graves, Long Cairns and Chambered Tombs

Decorated standing stone outside the burial chamber.

The chambered tomb which measures 8 feet across and 6 feet high, is D-shaped and entered by a roofed passage on the eastern side, 7–10 feet long, 6 feet high and 26 feet long. When this tomb was excavated, large quantities of burned and unburned bones were found. It may have been a site of human sacrifice as well as a burial chamber. Inside is a stone pillar about 3 feet 6 inches high with a smooth surface and it is almost perfectly circular in cross-section. Outside the burial chamber is a standing stone decorated with continuous zig-zags and pitted lines running over the top and down both sides. This is a cast of the original stone which can be seen in the National Museum of Wales, Cardiff.

When Sir Norman Lockyer visited this site in 1908 he observed that it was in a 'state of dilapidation' and his survey shows that the passage of the tomb was in line with the midsummer sunrise.

Location: Situated in a field 1 mile SE of Llanddaniel Fab, Anglesey, Caernarfonshire. It is well signposted off the A4080 and a path leads from a car park across fields to the monument – SH 508702 (114)

Gop y Goleuni Neolithic Barrow.

The Largest Prehistoric Monument in Wales
Gop y Goleuni on Gop Hill, overlooking the A5151, is a massive cairn made of limestone, 820 feet above sea level. This notable landmark is a Neolithic barrow and it is the second biggest man-made mound in Britain after Silbury Hill. According to Thomas Pennant, the eighteenth-century antiquarian, it was once known as Copa'rleni or Cop yr goleuni ('Mount of Lights'), as it was used as a beacon site in the early seventeenth century.

The mound is 60 feet in height, and covers an area of 100 yards by 68 yards. In 1886–7, Professor Boyd Dawkins dug a shaft into the centre of the cairn, down to the original ground level, and also made side tunnels at its base, but only some animal bones were found.

In a sepulchral cave situated below the tumulus were found fourteen skeletons in crouched positions, with their arms and legs drawn together and folded. It is of interest that the shape of their skulls showed two different periods of man, thought to be Neolithic and Early Bronze Age. Fragments of crude pottery, flint tools and bones of both wild and domesticated animals were also found.

Location: On Gop Hill, above Trelawnydd, and reached via a footpath off Llanasa Road, Flintshire – SJ 087801 (116)

6

Misconceptions and Preconceived Ideas

Archaeologists all over the world have realised that much of prehistory, as written in the existing text books, is inadequate: some of it quite simply wrong.

Professor Colin Renfrew

The earliest mention of the British megalithic monuments attributed their erection to the Danes of the ninth century, and Walter Charlton's *Chorea Gigantum*, published in 1643, states that Stonehenge was the ancient coronation place of the Danish kings. Later, the Romans were given credit for the erection of these monuments and it was John Aubrey (1626–1697) who first suggested that Stonehenge and other megalithic monuments were connected with the Druids.

He decided that both Stonehenge and Avebury Stone Circle were constructed before Saxon or Roman times, and that since the Druids were 'the most eminent order of priests among the Britaines, 'tis odds, but that these monuments were the temples of the priests of the most eminent order, viz, Druids, and it is strongly to be presumed that they are as ancient as those days.'

Aubrey was a pioneer archaeologist who is particularly noted for discovering the Avebury henge monument in 1649, and refers to it as a druidic temple in his *Monumenta Britannica*, which exists in manuscript form in the Bodleian Library, Oxford.

William Stukeley, who published a book on Stonehenge in 1740, agreed with Aubrey that the Druids must have been responsible for its construction. He was supported by his contemporary, John Wood, who in the same year wrote a *Description of Stanton Drew and Stonehenge*. Seven years later his *Choir Gawr Vulgarily called Stonehenge* was published and he interpreted it as an oracular lunar temple and gave his thoughts on the Druid philosophy.

Stukeley's work on Stonehenge was the first attempt to date the monument and he estimated that it had been built in 460 BC, which is now believed to have been too late by several thousand years.

Dr John Smith, in 1770, then wrote a book with the long title, *Choir Gawr, the Grand Orrery of the Ancient Druids, called Stonehenge, Astronomically Explained, and proved to be a Temple for Observing the Matanus of the Heavenly Bodies*. He stated that the Heel Stone, viewed from the centre of the temple, marked the sunrise point at the summer solstice and further claimed that the thirty pillars of the outer sarsen circle multiplied by the twelve zodiacal signs were intended to indicate the 360 days of the ancient solar year, while the inner circle of bluestones stood for the twenty-nine days and twelve hours of the lunar month.

Wansey in *Stonehenge*, published in 1796, commented that 'until we know the methods by which the ancient Druids calculated eclipses long before they happened, so as to make their astronomical observations with so much accuracy as Caesar maintains, we cannot explain the theoretical uses of Stonehenge.'

William Stukeley's portrayal of a 'British Druid'.

Misconceptions and Preconceived Ideas

The existence of the Druids had been confirmed in the writings of Julius Caesar, who had learned about them during his 'conquest' of Britain. He described them as men of great learning 'given to discussions of stars and their movements, the size of the universe and of the earth'.

Until the nineteenth century, British antiquarians firmly believed that Stonehenge and other megalithic monuments had been designed and built as temples by the Druids, the ancient Celtic scholar-priests, something of whose religion was known from the writings of Roman historians. It is certainly possible that the Druids used megaliths as sites for their own religious rituals, but the scant knowledge that we have of them in ancient texts suggests that they were only active a thousand years after the completion of Stonehenge, when its original purpose may have long been forgotten.

Eighteenth-century engraving depicting a Druid at Stonehenge.

Dating the Monuments

The Megaliths themselves cannot be dated accurately. Radiocarbon dating works only with matter that has once been alive but carbon dating of burial remains found at the foot of some British standing stones suggests they were erected some 2000 BC. Attempts at dating in places such as Brittany indicate a similar or sometimes earlier date. The consensus of archaeological opinion seems to be that the British stone circles were in some way associated with the religious life of the late Neolithic and early Bronze Age peoples.

During the Neolithic period – 4,000 BC to 2,000 BC – the population of Britain would have totalled no more than 20,000. The Bronze Age followed not far behind the New Stone Age, and with it came new peoples who are known as the Beaker folk, who crossed from the mainland of Europe in about 2,000 BC and landed along the eastern and southern coasts of Britain, generally penetrating inland. They are named after their particular kind of pottery, the beaker. These were small red-brown drinking cups ranging from 5 to 7 inches in height which were placed in their graves.

The Beaker people buried their dead in single graves which they covered with a round mound or barrow of earth and stone, whereas the cromlech builders used to bury large numbers of peoples in their stone tombs.

One thing that is conveniently overlooked is that there is no firm evidence to show the places of habitation used by the builders of these large and very heavy stone monuments. One would expect that the ancient people who skilfully handled masses of stone weighing 20 tons or more would have no difficulty in erecting a large stone dwelling for at least one of their leaders, but it seems that such buildings were never constructed.

The full area of ignorance is not mapped: we are at present only exploring its fringes.

J.D. Bernal

Example of a Beaker drinking cup found at Penderyn.

7
Markings on the Stones

Scattered well nigh all over the world, at any rate over the Megalithic world, are found a series of markings which have been called cup and ring markings. They are only found on megaliths or on objects belonging to the megalithic culture.

Gilbert Stone

Cup and Ring Markings

Cup marks or small circular hollows are found cut into some prehistoric stones and are estimated to be 4000–5000 years old which dates them to the Neolithic or Bronze Ages. Known as petroglyphs or rock art, they can be found on stones worldwide and they have been the subject of endless archaeological debate. They vary from simple hollows about 5 inches across to those 6 inches across. Sometimes they are surrounded by a ring or rings which have a groove running through them. The original meaning of these symbols is now lost and they merely provide a link with our prehistoric ancestors.

Cup and ring markings.

They can be found on dolmens and passage tombs in France, North Africa, Corsica, Palestine, Germany, Scandinavia as well as Great Britain. It is quite amazing that such an unusual design could have been conceived independently by so many different races thousands of miles apart.

There is perhaps an early reference to these markings in the ancient *Triads of the Islands of Britain*, mentioning the stones of Gwidden-Ganhebon, on which 'one could read the arts and sciences of the world', and to the 'astronomer Gwydon-ap Don', who was buried at Caernarfon 'under a Stone of Enigmas'.

The first drawing known of a cup-and-ring marking was made by Colonel Montgomery in 1785, and showed the cover of a cist found at Coilsfield in Ayrshire, decorated with a spiral, cup and six concentric circles.

The largest number discovered on a single stone in Wales is on the capstone of a dolmen called Bachwen Clynnog at Clynnog near Caernarfon (SH 4076497). It displays 110 cup markings, but unfortunately these are not clearly visible now due to weathering. They show up well on photographs taken in the late nineteenth century.

Welsh wind and rain will erode even the hardest stone so it is not surprising that such man-made markings cut more than two thousand years ago are now hard to see. The finest examples are of course those that can be found inside a cromlech or burial barrow for they have been well protected from the elements. The best example in Wales of such markings is inside Bryn Celli Ddu, which is situated in the Parish of Llandaniel Fab, Anglesey (SH 508702). One of the markings is an incised spiral on a pillar stone about 5 feet high which stands inside the chamber. It is similar in form to markings found at the New Grange monument in Meath, Ireland.

George Tate commented in 1865:

> Look at the extent of their distribution, from one extremity of Britain to the other, and even into Ireland; and say, what could induce tribes, living hundreds of miles apart and even separated by the sea, to use precisely the same symbols, save to express some religious sentiment, or to aid in the performance of some superstitious rites.

What is the purpose of the cup-and-ring marks? Bishop Browne, who in 1919 studied such markings on recumbent stones in Scotland, found that many of them were accurately arranged to form patterns of various constellations of the heavenly bodies, but in every case the image was reversed as if the stars were reflected in a mirror.

Another theory is that they indicate the locations of nearby underground springs. It would seem that the prehistoric people who chiselled them into so many rocks with such evident care and skill must have had some object in doing so. Perhaps one day their meaning will be identified.

> *There is an affinity between these cups and the nature of the stars. A star is a generator and transmitter of cosmic energy in spiral form. These cups could be used as micros-cosmic examples of spiral-star energies.*
>
> John Foster Forbes

A Good Example of a Cup-Marked Capstone

Clynnog Dolmen has a capstone 9 feet long and it is of particular interest that the greater part of the upper surface is covered with artificial cup-shaped hollows. There are approximately 110 in number and they do not appear to be arranged in any particular order. It would seem from the number of locations where these markings have been discovered that they are neither merely ornamental nor freaks of nature, and that the prehistoric people who chiselled them into so many rocks with such evident care and skill must have had some object in doing so.

Location: Near Clynnog Fawr, off A499, Caernarfonshire – SH 4076 4947 (115)

Cup marks on the capstone of Clynnog Cromlech.

Megaliths of Wales: Mysterious Sites in the Landscape

Decorated with Many Cup Marks

Trellyffant Burial Chamber has two compartments and the capstone which measures 6 feet 10 inches by 6 feet is decorated with over thirty cup marks. According to the twelfth-century chronicler Giraldus Cambrensis, the name of this cromlech translates as 'Toad's Town' because the chieftain buried inside it was eaten by toads. Inside the nearby farmhouse used to be a black marble toad dating from the time of James I.

Location: 2 miles north of Nevern, west of B4582, Pembrokeshire – SN 083426 (145)

The capstone of Trellyfant Dolmen is decorated with over thirty cup marks.

A Good Example of a Cup-Marked Stone

Maen Catwg (Catwg's Stone) is a squat boulder measuring 9 feet by 6 feet. It is named after St Catwg who spent some time in this vicinity during the sixth century. There are several cup marks, varying in size and depth, to be seen on the top of the stone. They are dish and conical-shaped holes up to 5 inches in diameter.

Location: In a field west of Heol Adam (Roman road) and half a mile north of the Roman fort of Gelligaer, Glamorgan – ST 127974 (171)

Maen Catwg (Catwg's Stone).

Markings on the Stones

Possible Cup Markings

Corwen Cross (near the tower of Corwen Church) stands on an elliptical base 12 inches thick. On the surface of this stone are seven depressions which seem to resemble cup markings. They are arranged in an irregular pattern and differ in size, although they are similar in shape. It is possible that the base of this cross was once the capstone of a cromlech and was removed centuries ago from its original site to be reused for its present purpose.

Location: Corwen Church, Merionethshire – SJ 078434 (135)

Corwen Cross.

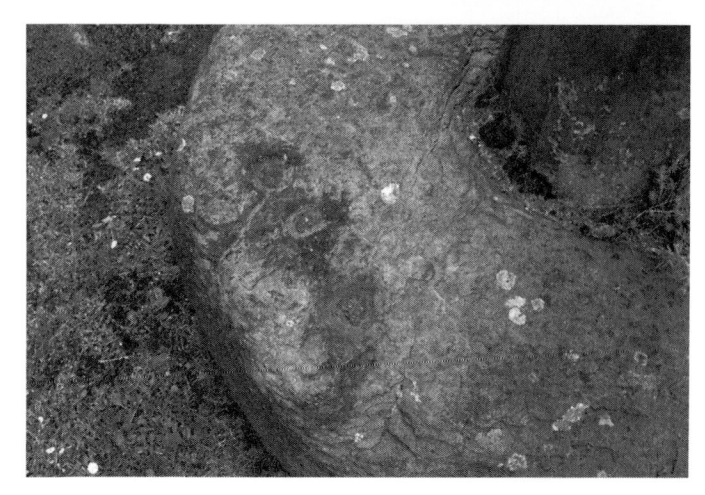

Possible cup marks on the base of Corwen Cross.

Roman Inscriptions

The Romans utilised a few of the large prehistoric standing stones for their own purposes and a good example is the following one.

Maen Madoc is believed to be a Bronze Age standing stone that was later used by the Romans as a road marker and then as a memorial stone during the Dark Ages. It is 11 feet high, 2½ feet wide and 1¼ feet thick with a Latin inscription, dating from the fourth century, on the western side. The crude Latin capitals read downwards and some of them are reversed. There is no parallel Ogham inscription, unlike some of the other inscribed stones in the Brecon area. The inscription reads:

DERVAC FILIUST IVST JACIT
(The Stone) of Dervacus, son of Justus

The first letter D is reversed and the R with the bottom right-hand stroke is horizontal. In FiLIUS the F and I are conjoined, both the Ls with the first strokes obliquely slanting, the terminal S reversed. The identity of Dervacus is obscure and the names do not figure in the genealogies of the royal family of Brycheiniog. The words *Hic Iacit* (Here lies) imply that he was a Christian. The origin of the name Maen Madoc is not known but it is of interest that there is a Castell Madoc about 4 miles due north, near the Senni river and a Nant Madoc about 2 miles further south.

The site was investigated by the Ministry of Works in 1940 and it was decided that the stone had at one time fallen and been re-erected about 20 yards from its original position. A few feet behind it a large pit was uncovered which may have been the grave of Dervacus.

Location: On the side of the Roman road known as Sarn Helen on an exposed and often windy crest. Sarn Helen joins the mountain road from Defynnog to Ystradfellte nearly 2 miles to the south of Maen Llia and it is about 1 mile to walk from that point to the site of this stone, Brecknockshire – SN 918157 (160)

Maen Madoc.

Markings on the Stones

Strange Markings

The Grooved Stone

The Queen Stone is situated just outside Wales in Herefordshire but has been included because it is very unusual. Composed of sandstone conglomerate, it has deep grooves about 2 inches wide and up to 7 inches deep on each of its four sides and a single cup mark depression on the eastern face. The grooves stop at the old ground level and excavation has shown that the stone projects downwards to a depth of about 8 feet

Location: In a loop of the River Wye, west of Huntsham Bridge, Herefordshire – SO 562182 (162)

The Queen Stone has deep grooves on all four sides.

Carreg Waun Llech.

A Stone with Strange Holes

Carreg Waun Llech stands on marshy ground on Llangynidr Mountain, about 50 yards from the road. It is a well-weathered slab of limestone standing about 8 feet high, 4 feet wide and 16 inches thick. There are strange lines of holes on its west and east sides, but the other two sides are smooth. It now serves as a boundary marker between the Llangynidr and Llangattock communities.

From this location there are excellent views across the Usk Valley to the Black Mountains.

Location: Near a minor road on Mynydd Llangynidr, Brecknockshire – SO 164175 (161)

Markings on the Stones

The Llyswen Stone.

The Llyswen Leaning Stone
This large standing stone is about 7 feet 8 inches high and 2 feet 7 inches wide and 1 foot 9 inches thick. It leans at an angle of about 30 degrees. On its south-western face and about 4 feet above the ground are about 30 small hollows, which may be cup marks.

Location: In the middle of a field between the River Wye and Llangoed Castle Hotel at Llyswen, Brecknockshire – SO 124398 (161)

> *The retrieval of these forgotten things from oblivion in some sort resembles the art of a conjurer.*
>
> John Aubrey

Christianised Standing Stones

The early Christians converted some of the large standing stones by carving crosses on the upright faces to show that they had been taken over by the local church. One of the best examples of this is a stone which stands in the churchyard on the south side of Bridell Church in Ceredigion (SN 177421). It is 7 feet tall and elegant in shape, tapering uniformly to the top. It is formed of the porphyrite greenstone of the Preseli Hills and has a large equal-armed cross cut inside a circle on its northen face. In addition, it has Ogam letters cut into its vertical edges and there are cup markings on its surface, so this is a unique specimen of a large standing stone being used by three separate cultures. The Ogam inscription reads: 'Nettasagru Maqui Muoci Breci', which has been translated to mean: Nettasagus son of the descendants of Brecii. It was most likely carved in the fifth or sixth century AD.

The best recorded prehistoric standing stones bearing Ogam inscriptions are found in Southern Ireland and it would seem that none are known to exist in England. Ogam is the more ancient method of spelling the word but in modern Irish it is spelt Ogham.

In the Dark Ages, those prehistoric stones which were near churches were very often taken down and replaced with a Christian preaching cross, to which there were later added raised stone pedestals.

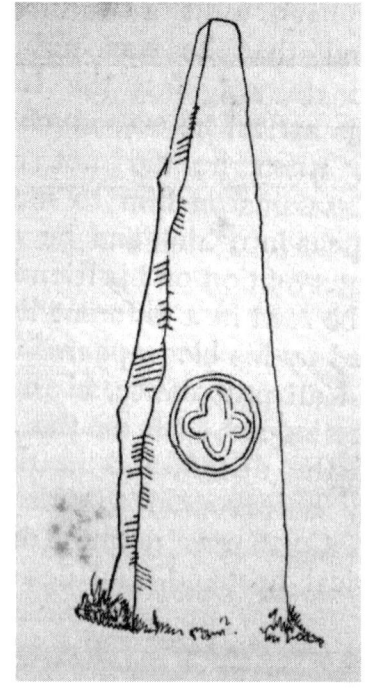

The Bridell Stone is carved with a cross and an Ogam inscription.

Markings on the Stones

The Corbalenecus Stone.

A Memorial to Balencus
A prehistoric standing stone inscribed with the Latin inscription: COR BALENCUS JUCIT ORDOVS which translates as 'The heart of Balencus the Ordovical lies here.' He was probably from the territory of the Ordovicium tribe in mid-Wales.

When the Reverend Henry Jenkins excavated beneath this stone in 1850 he discovered an urn containing ashes, coins of silver and bronze, and a gold chain of the reign of the Roman Emperor Vespasian. Perhaps a battle was fought near herè against the invading Romans in which Balencus was killed, and an existing standing stone became his memorial.

Location: Near Penbryn, between Cardigan and Newquay, Cardiganshire – SN 288514 (145)

Megaliths of Wales: Mysterious Sites in the Landscape

Maen Achwyfan.

A Tall Cross that May have been Fashioned from a Standing Stone
It is possible that this wheel cross was fashioned from a prehistoric standing stone. Known as Maen Achwyfan ('The Stone of Lamentation'), it is 12 feet tall and is carved with ornate Celtic designs on all sides. It is also called St Cwyfan's Stone and according to *Gibson's Camden* it was mentioned in an old deed dated 1388.

Location: At the junction of some ancient tracks in the corner of a field, 1 mile west of Whitford, Flintshire – SJ 129787 (116)

Markings on the Stones

The Roihi Stone.

An Early Christian Memorial Inscription
On Gelligaer Common to the east of Carn Bugail round cairn and standing on the side of an ancient trackway is a standing stone which is 8 feet 6 inches tall and slopes at a crazy angle. Years ago a Latin inscription could be seen on its eastern face: it read TEFROIHI (the Stone of Roihi). This was defaced at some time before 1862, leaving just the letters IHI. These were obliterated some years later by a group of colliers. A local belief that treasure may be hidden under the stone may have led to someone trying to uproot it and this may explain why it leans so much.

Location: On the north side of the road between Bedlinog and Rhymney, Glamorgan – SO 1040349 (171)

An old photograph of 'the Maiden Stone' in its original location.

Maen y Morwynion (The Maiden's Stone)
This stone used to stand beside a Roman road leading to Y Gaer Fort, just outside Brecon, and the above photograph shows it in its original position. It is possible that this was originally a prehistoric standing stone and the carving on it represents a Roman soldier and his wife. The stone, now much weathered by wind and rain, is in Brecon Museum.

Location: Brecon Museum, Brecon, Brecknockshire.

8

Churches Built on Megalithic Sites

The early Christian practice of taking over and reconsecrating the sites of pagan shrines and temples has ensured that virtually every old church stands on a place of long pre-Christian sanctity.

John Michell

Under the rule of Constantine, the tendency was to destroy heathen temples and their idols, but by the Edict of Theodosius (AD 392) pagan shrines were to be dedicated as Christian churches. Later an Edict of Honorius (AD 408) forbade the demolition of heathen temples in areas of high population.

The Council of Tours in 567 recommended the excommunication of those who persisted in worshipping trees, stones or fountains. Pope Gregory the Great in 601 sent a letter to Abbot Mellitus, who was then about to visit Britain, containing the following statement:

> When (by God's help) you come to our most reverend brother, Bishop Augustine, I want you to tell him how earnestly I have been pondering over the affairs of the English: I have come to the conclusion that the temples of the idols in England should not on any account be destroyed. Augustine must smash the idols, but the temples themselves should be sprinkled with holy water and altars set up in them in which relics are to be enclosed. For we ought to take advantage of well-built temples by purifying them from devil-worship and dedicating them to the service of the true God. In this way, I hope the people (seeing that their temples are not destroyed) will leave their idolatry and yet continue to frequent the places as formerly, so coming to know and revere the true God.

We may wonder now, just how many of our prehistoric stone monuments were completely destroyed and how many ancient churches still have the remains of these stones in their foundations.

Examples of circular churchyards in Wales can be seen at the following churches: Llanelidan, Efenechtyd, Llandyrnog, Tremeirchion, Cilcaen, Llanarmon, Cerrig-y-drudion, Bettws Gwerfil Goch, Llangelynin, Llaneltud, Pennant Melangell, Llaniltud and Kilgwrrwg.

A Centre of Pagan Worship
St John's Church at Yspytty Cynfyn has a circular churchyard with the remnants of a Bronze Age stone circle built into part of its surrounding wall. Only five large upright stones remain of the circle and only one (at the north) is in its original position. Two of them have been moved to serve as gateposts at the east entrance to the churchyard, but the other two stones are probably in their original positions. These stones indicate that the site was once a centre of pagan worship long before the church was built. Yspytty means a hospital or hospice and there was probably a hospice of Strata Florida Abbey here during the Middle Ages.

Location: In the Parish of Llanbadarn Fawr, Powys, 2½ miles from Devil's Bridge on the A4120, Cardiganshire – SN 752791

Remains of a stone circle at Yspytty Cynfyn Church.

Churches Built on Megalithic Sites

There are many churches throughout Britain which have circular churchyards and these could have once been the sites of stone circles. At Llanfair Pwllgwyngyll, Anglesey, a menhir was found beneath the pulpit of the church. It is significant that Pope Gregory in AD 601 commanded Orlygus '... to build a church wherever he found pagan stone circles or menhirs.' St Patrick even established his cathedral at Armagh in Ireland on the edge of a Bronze Age stone circle, and streets mark its boundaries.

A Christianised Site

The 'Thumb-Shaped Stone' which can be seen in the north porch of Corwen Church is also known as the 'pointed stone in the cold corner'. It would seem that the church was built next to the standing stone which at a later date was incorporated into the wall of the church porch. The stone can only be seen from the outside as the interior wall of the porch has been covered in plaster.

There is a local tradition that 'all attempts to build the church in any other location than where stood the Cerrig y Big yn y fach newlyd (i.e. 'the pointed stone in the cold corner') were frustrated by the influence of adverse powers.

Location: Corwen Church, Merionethshire – SJ 078434 (125)

Examples of prehistoric standing stones in churchyards can be found at the following locations: Llanwrthwl, Powys (SN 975637); Llanarth, Powys (SN 423577); Llanbadarn Fawr, Powys (SN 598810); Llandewi Brefi, Ceredigion (SN 664553); Llandawke, Pembrokeshire (SN 283112); Llanbedr y Cenin, Gwynedd (SH 585269); Llangain, Gwynedd (SH 297289); Maentwrog, Gwynedd (SH 664406); Bryngwyn, Powys (SO 187496).

The 'Thumb-Shaped Stone'.

Megaliths of Wales: Mysterious Sites in the Landscape

Standing stone beside Llanwrthwl Church.

Another Christianised Site
In Llanwrthwl churchyard, near Rhayader, is a large standing stone close to the church porch. It is 6 feet high and was here long before the church was built.

Location: Llanwrthwl, south of Rhayader on the A470, Radnorshire – SN 975637 (141)

9

Some Fascinating Legends

We may reject legends if we please, but history would be incomplete without them, for they represent the temper of the people by whom great institutions were founded and among whom they flourished.

Phillott

Legends have been attached to many standing stones to account for their existence. Some stories suggest that they have the ability to come alive at certain times of the year, to uproot themselves from the ground and start walking, running or dancing. The relevant times for the stones to come to life is at midnight, cock crow, sunrise or noon, while others specify particular times of the year, such as New Year, Easter, Midsummer, or All Hallows' Eve.

It is said to be bad luck to disturb a standing stone in a circle and that it may be impossible to count the number of stones present in the circle, for you get a different total each time you try. There are also legends that stones in a circle were once human beings who were turned to stone as a result of some misdemeanour, such as dancing on a Sunday or dancing through the night until sunrise. This seems to point to some memory of the ritual use of these sites in ancient times. The stones at the Merry Maidens stone circle in Cornwall are said to be musicians who played faster and faster until they became petrified with exhaustion. There are also stones which are reputed to have been thrown to their sites from locations some distance away by giants, the Devil or King Arthur.

Tradition has it that at certain times of the day or year certain standing stones spring to life and go down to a nearby stream or river to wash, drink or swim. Such examples are Maen Llia and the Fish Stone, which can be found in the Brecon Beacons National Park.

It was once believed that anyone who planned to visit the site of a 'wandering megalith during its absence, in order to seek treasure buried at its base, would not live to see the next day!

Apparently, it was once considered unlucky to sleep on the massive capstone of Tinkinswood burial chamber on 'the three spirit nights' of May Day Eve, St John's Eve (23 June), and Midwinter Eve. If you took no notice of this advice, then you might be found dead the next day, go mad, or become a brilliant poet. A similar tradition is attached to spending a night on the summit of Cadair Idris.

Arthurian Associations

> *During the centuries the legend grew in richness and wonder and Arthur himself somehow got submerged into it.*
>
> Rosemary Sutcliff

The prehistoric monuments of Wales have a variety of names, all of which can be said to be very old, and their origins have been lost in the mists of time. Descriptive words in the Welsh language are often used such as Maen Hir (Long Stone) or Maen Llwyd (Grey Stone), but very often the English equivalent is now used instead.

It is also interesting that so many of these megalithic sites have become associated with King Arthur, such as Arthur's Stone on Cefn Bryn in Gower. He, of course, was a great sixth-century folk hero who became credited with amazing deeds which provided an interesting explanation for the existence or shape of a particular monument.

John Williams explains the Arthurian association of such sites as follows:

> The Great Bear is the name of the well-known northern constellation of seven prominent stars, which are also called Ursa Major or The Plough, and it continually circles the present North Pole star which is the nearest thing to a fixed point in the universe.

Some Fascinating Legends

The Welsh Arth Fawr or Great Bear has connections with the polar regions of the northern skies, which go back beyond any period of recorded time in Welsh history. In Welsh folklore, Ursa Major was called Aradr Arthur, that is Arthur's Plough, while the constellation of stars we now call Lyra was known as Telyn Arthur or Arthur's Harp. The prominent line of stars which are said to form the belt of Orion were called Llath Arthur or Arthur's Wand.

It is necessary to look back into the dim past before the time of King Arthur for the Great Arthur whose name is so often associated with our prehistoric stone monuments and this, of course is very difficult. There are no written records of such early periods but fortunately some help can be gained from the Welsh language, which is the oldest in Europe. Students of etymology realise that the important part of any language is the spoken word as phonetics change less than written words. In Welsh, Arth Fawr means Great Bear and the two words need only the slightest phonetic change to become Arthur.

There must have been some very early Welsh stories relating to the origins of these Arthurian groups of stars which were probably suppressed by leaders of later cultures because they were inconsistent with their views. These early stories may have told something about the uses of Polar Forces and there seem to be a few vague references to this in some of the earliest Arthurian legends.

Thus it would seem that wherever a megalithic monument is named after Arthur the name in Welsh (Arth Fawr) means Great Bear, and this may be a clue that the earth's energy system relates to polar magnetism. It is only comparatively recently that modern man has discovered radio waves and X-rays, so is it possible that prehistoric man discovered something analogous which is still unknown to us?

There are 200 prehistoric sites with Arthurian connections. These appear as widely dispersed as Argylshire and Berkshire, Dumfriesshire and Hertfordshire, Cumberland and Surrey, Westmorland and Glamorganshire.

Paul Screeton

The Wonder of the World on Gower

Arthur's Stone, prominently situated on Cefn Bryn, above Reynoldstone, is a chambered tomb dating to approximately 2,500 BC. It stand at the centre of a ring cairn 75 feet in diameter. The huge capstone is a quartz conglomerate boulder and weighs about 24 tons. It is 14 feet long, 7 feet 2 inches in depth and 6 feet 6 inches in breadth and is supported by four of the ten uprights. The capstone is split into two pieces and part of it can be seen lying on the ground to the left. Taliesin Williams, the over-zealous archdruid who often wrote under his bardic name Ab Iolo, commented that St David split the stone with his sword to prove that it was not sacred.

Also known as Maen Ceti, this cromlech has been described as the 'wonder of the World on Gower'. The raising of the huge stone onto its supports has been summed up in ancient records as one of 'the three arduous undertakings accomplished in Britain'. Hence the proverb Mal gwaith Maen Cetti – 'Like the labour of the Stone of Cetti'. However, it is quite possible that the boulder was not actually raised but instead carefully excavated and then underpinned by the placement, one at a time, of the supporting stones.

More strange tales and legends are associated with this ancient stone monument than any other megalithic site in Wales. The Reverend J. Evans stated in 1804 that a stream ebbing and flowing with the tide beneath Arthur's Stone was celebrated as Fynnon Fair or Lady's Well.

Nineteenth-century engraving of Arthur's Stone, Gower.

Some Fascinating Legends

Part of the capstone is lying on the ground to the left.

The massive capstone is underpinned by supporting stones.

Today there are no visible signs of a spring or well at the dolmen and, as it is at an altitude of 482 feet, any spring beneath the structure is unlikely to be affected by the tide! This tradition is best explained by the fact that the hollow in which the monument stands can easily collect surface water which then gradually soaks away.

A popular story claims that the large stone is a pebble that King Arthur found in his shoe when he was on his way to fight the Battle of Camlann. He plucked it out and threw it a great distance to this spot on Cefn Bryn.

The legend about Arthur's Stone going down to the sea to drink appears to have been first recorded in *Some Folk-lore of South Wales*, in 1898, where the author mentions that it is said that on certain nights of the year it goes down to Port Eynon, a few miles away, to drink of the sea.

Another legend which can be found in *Folklore, Myths and Legends of Britain* (1973) mentions local girls placing a honey cake soaked in milk on the stone at midnight when the moon is full. They would then crawl the stone three times on their hands and knees, hoping to see their sweethearts. If they appeared, their fidelity was proved, but if not, then the girls knew that the boys did not intend to marry them. However, it is doubtful that any self-respecting Gower girl would be prepared to come forward to confirm that she had performed this ritual on a moonlit night.

The fame of Arthur's Stone is such that a force of Breton soldiers en route from Milford Haven to the fifteenth-century Battle of Bosworth made a 60-mile detour to see it.

Maen Ceti was excavated in 1870 by the famous Egyptologist Sir Gardiner Wilkinson, who also identified the remains of a stone avenue leading to the site. It was one of the first sites to be protected under the Ancient Monuments Act of 1882.

Location: A well-trodden footpath leads from a parking area on the road from Cilibion to Reynoldston where it crosses Cefn Bryn, Gower, Glamorgan – SN 491905 (159)

Some Fascinating Legends

Maen y Cleddau – 'the Sword Stones'.

Marks Made by Arthur's Sword
Maen y Cleddau (The Sword Stones) is a split rock which can be seen standing in an enclosure called 'The Field of the Stones'. On each segment of rock is a shape resembling the blade of a sword. Legend tells how Arthur threw his sword against the rock and made the marks.

Location: Near Sylfaen Farm, above Barmouth, Merionethshire – SH 631188 (124)

A Spear Thrown by a Gaint
Ffon y Cawr (Giant's Staff) is also known as Arthur's Spear and this long needle-shaped stone which stands 7 feet 3 inches high slopes towards the east. There is a story of a giant (sometimes Arthur) who, standing on Pen y Gaer sent his dog to bring in sheep from Tal y Fan but the dog went to shelter in the nearby Maen y Bardd cromlech. The giant threw his stick after it, which stuck in the ground to form this slim standing stone.

Location: To the west of Rowen, Caernarfonshire – SH 738717 (115)

Ffon y Cawr.

Megaliths of Wales: Mysterious Sites in the Landscape

Where Arthur's Sons were Said to be Killed

Cerrig Meibion Arthur (The Stones of the Sons of Arthur) is the name of two stones about 8 feet tall, which stand about 3 yards apart and are aligned east-west. They point to the equinox sunrise and are said to commemorate King Arthur's sons who were killed by the Twrch Trwyth, a wild boar that had originally swum over from Ireland. This story is told in great detail in the Mabinogion tale of 'Kulhwch and Olwen', and it was here that Arthur and his men had one of their running fights with the great boar Twrch Trwyth.

Location: South-east of Ty Newydd Farm, on open ground north of the Mynachlogddu to Rosebush Lane, Pembrokeshire – SN 118310 (145).

Cerrig Meibion Arthur.

Some Fascinating Legends

Bedd Arthur (Arthur's Grave) in the Preseli Mountains.

One of Many Places where Arthur is Said to be Buried
Bedd Arthur (Arthur's Grave) is an oval-shaped stone ring with truncated ends. The largest diameter is about 70 feet and the stones visible are placed at irregular intervals. There are sixteen stones arranged in two groups of eight and one stone positioned in the centre of each end. In height, the stones range from 3 feet to 10 inches.

Location: In the Preseli Mountains to the north of Mynachlog Ddu village, Pembrokeshire – SN 131325 (145)

St Cybi's Stone.

Associated with Saints

St Cybi's Campsite
St Cybi's Stone is 6 feet in height and there is a local tradition that it marks the spot where the wandering Cornish saint Cybi 'pitched his tent' in the sixth century. The local ruler, King Ithel, tried to have Cybi and his followers removed from his land, but he was no match for the saint's powers. His horse dropped dead and he was struck blind. He lay before the saint in such dejection that Cybi took pity on him and not only restored his sight but also brought his horse back to life. In gratitude King Ithel presented Cybi with a handbell and land on which to build a church.

Location: In the middle of a field between Llangybi Church and the River Usk, Monmouthshire – ST 381965 (171)

Some Fascinating Legends

St Peter is Said to have Preached Here
Peterstone, on the north side of the A40 opposite Llanhamlach Church, is a small rectangular standing stone which has been protected by a low wooden fence. It is greyish-green in colour and about 4 feet 6 inches tall and 2 feet square. There is an unlikely tradition that St Peter once preached at this spot and not surprisingly the mansion opposite is called Peterstone Court.

Location: Llanhamlach, on the north side of the A40 Brecknockshire – SO 089267 (160)

St Peter's Stone.

Associated with St Illtud
Ty Illtud is a cromlech in which the top stone is oval and flat, 2½ yards long by 1¾ yards broad and slopes towards the north. The inner chamber is about 6 feet by 5 feet wide and about 3 feet high. On the right-hand side are a number of small crosses and other marks scratched on the inner surface of the upright stones. The end of the chamber is closed by a long transverse slab like the others. Further stones towards the north of the entrance suggest another capstone once existed.

It used to be claimed that this Neolithic burial chamber was used as a hermitage by St Illtud and it was even suggested that this sixth-century holy man was responsible for carving the crosses and other marks on the stones. However, it is most likely that they were made during Victorian times.

Location: In a field (private land), opposite Manest Farm, 1km east of Llanhamlach, Brecknockshire – SO 098263 (160)

Ty Illtud burial chamber.

125

Remains of Bedd Gwyl Illtud.

Also Associated with St Illtud
Bedd Gwyl Illtud is the remains of a dolmen consisting of just two stones in a hollow. According to local tradition it is the grave of St Illtud. However, he is more likely to have been buried at the nearby ancient church of Llanilltud (now demolished), which he founded in the sixth century.

Location: On Mynydd Illtud, Brecknockshire – SN 975264 (160)

Stones Thrown from Afar

Numerous legends describe how standing stones were thrown to their particular sites by either a giant, the Devil, a local saint, or King Arthur, from a location many miles away. Before dismissing these stories one should carefully check that the geological content of the particular monolith is not the same as the rock at the place from which it is supposed to have been thrown. If the ancient builders could move the famous Bluestones from the Preseli Hills to Stonehenge about 200 miles away, then it is reasonable to assume that they could move large prehistoric standing stones from their place of origin, 20 or 30 miles, to where they now stand and have since stood for thousands of years.

Some Fascinating Legends

Maen Twrog.

Thrown by St Twrog

Maen Twrog which stands near the door of Maentwrog Church is also known as St Twrog's Stone and is associated with a sixth-century holy man who was a close companion of St Beuno. According to a local tale the stone was thrown here by St Twrog from Moelwyn Bach 3 miles to the north in order to destroy a pagan altar. The marks of his fingers and thumb can still be seen on the stone, which is 5 feet high and 2 feet wide. It was undoubtedly here long before the first Christian church was founded on this pagan site.

Inside the church is a stained-glass window depicting St Twrog holding a book in one hand and his other hand on the stone.

Location: Maentwrog, A496, Merioneth – SH 664406 (124)

The Devil's Quoit.

Thrown by the Devil in a Fit of Temper!
The Devil's Quoit is a 6-feet high standing stone which is said to have been hurled across the Bristol Channel to this spot from Portishead, Somerset, by the Devil in a fit of temper.

Location: In the middle of a field west of Llanfihangel Rogiet Church, Monmouthshire – ST 448876 (171)

Some Fascinating Legends

Thrown by a Giantess

St Meulig's Cross is 7 feet high, 3 feet wide and 10 inches thick. It may originally have been a prehistoric standing stone that has been converted into a Celtic cross. The plain cross on one side dates back to the sixth or seventh century and the more intricately decorated cross on the other face was carved in the eleventh century. Originally it stood high on the Begwyn Hills to the north-west of Llowes and for some unknown reason it was removed and erected in this churchyard, where it stood for 800 years. In more recent times it was uprooted and taken inside the church for safety.

This cross is also known as Malwalbee's Pebble after a mythical character based on Matilda de Valery, who was married to William de Breos, the Norman lord of Abergavenny during the time of King John. It is claimed that Malwalbee was a giantess who was carrying stones in her apron in order to build Hay Castle when one of the stones fell into her shoe. At first she didn't notice it, but when it began to annoy her she plucked it out and threw it across the River Wye to land near Llowes Church, about 3 miles away.

Location: Inside Llowes Church, Radnorshire – SO 192417 (148)

St Meulig's Cross.

Llech Idris.

Thrown by Idris Gawr
Llech Idris is 10 feet high, 4½ feet broad and 1 foot thick. It is said to have been thrown here by Idris Gawr of Welsh legend, who gave his name to Cader Idris and probably evolved out of an actual personage. There certainly lived, in about 600, an Idris, son of Gwyddno, and descendant of Meirion who gave his name to the district of Meirionydd between the Dovey and the Mawddach. He was probably the Idris who was slain in around 632 in the 'Slaughter of the Severn'. The stone does not necessarily mark his grave but is traditionally associated with him.

Location: West of Mynydd Bach, off the A470, SE of Bronaber, Merionethshire – SH 731310 (124)

Some Fascinating Legends

Coetan Arthur (Arthur's Quoit.)

Side view of Arthur's Quoit.

Thrown by Arthur
Coetan Arthur can be seen on top of Carn Arthur, an outcrop about 30 feet high on the south slopes of Mynydd Preseli. It is a rocking stone known as Arthur's Quoit. This large stone is said to have been hurled by King Arthur from Duffryn 2 miles away.

Location: Carn Arthur, Preseli Mountains, Pembrokeshire king – SN 135324 (145)

Carreg Myrddin.

A Stone Associated with Merlin the Magician
Carreg Myrddin stands 5 feet high and is 4 feet 6 inches broad at the base. There is a tradition that Merlin once prophesied that a raven would one day drink a man's blood off this stone. A remarkable coincidence is said to have taken place here in the nineteenth century, when a young man hunting for treasure was digging on one side of the stone to get to its base. The earth gave way and the stone fell, crushing him to death. The owner of the field arranged for the stone to be put back in its original position.

Location: In a field called Parc-ymaen-Llwyd at the foot of Merlin's Hill, near Carmarthen – SN 453215 (159)

Some Fascinating Legends

Llech y Drybedd.

Thrown by St Samson

Llech y Drybedd (Stone of the Three Graves) is a dolmen with a large triangular-shaped capstone which is supposed to have been thrown to this spot by St Samson from Carn Ingli. The capstone, which is 9 feet 5 inches long by 9 feet broad by 4 feet thick, is supported by three uprights 4 feet high. A fourth upright lies prostrate.

Location: Beside a footpath, off the Newport to Moylgrove road, Pembrokeshire – SN 101432 (145)

A List of Throwing Legends

The following twenty legends relate to the ancient Welsh megaliths being thrown to their present positions:

(1) Carreg Samson at Llanbadarn Fawr (SN 598810) was said to have been thrown into the churchyard by St Samson from Pen Dinas.

(2) Llech Gron, near Nebo in Llansantfraed (SN 542649), was said to have been carried away by the Devil to the top of Tricrug Mountain and then thrown back to its present position.

(3) Carreg Samson, near Penlan in Llanfihangel Lledrod (SN 655697), was launched from Uwch Mynydd by a giant.

(4) Barclodiad-y-Gawres or 'The Giantess's Apronful', a dolmen carn in Caerhun, Gwynedd (SH 716717) consists of stones dropped by two giants travelling to the island of Mona (Anglesey).

(5) A slender standing stone variously known as Ffon y Cawr, The Giant's Stick or Arthur's Spear, at Caerhun, Gwynedd (SH 739717), is supposed to have been thrown by a giant to this spot from Tal y Fan or Pen-y-Gaer.

(6) Coetan Arthur Cromlech, Ystumcegid Isaf in Llanystumdwy, Gwynedd (SH 498413), is supposed to have been thrown by King Arthur from a hill near Beddgelert.

(7) Coetan Arthur Cromlech near Mynydd Cefn Amlwch at Penllech, Gwynedd (SH 230346), which Arthur Gawr or Arthur the Giant cast from Carn Madryn, a hill a few miles away.

(8) Post-y-Wiber or 'Post of the Dragon' near Aber Rhiadr in Llanrhaidr-ym-Mochnant (see page 140), was supposed to have come from Cwm Clothy, near the waterfall, and was used for ridding the district of a dragon which had two haunts; one at Pengarnedd and the other at Bwlch Sychtyn in Llansillin Parish, adjoining on the north-east.

Some Fascinating Legends

(9) A maenhir near the school at Llanrhaidr-ym-Mochnant (see page…), which once did duty as a lamppost being 10 feet high. Tradition says that it was brought from Rhos Maes Criafal in Maengwynydd about 2 miles to the north.

(10) Carreg March Arthur, near Llanfernes Bridge at Mold, Flintshire (SJ 202626), is said to have been impressed with the hoof of King Arthur's horse when he landed here after leaping from the summit of Moel Farmmau. This is in direct alignment with the site of a destroyed standing stone in a field called Dol yr Orsedd at Pentrehobyn near Mold (SJ 245627).

(11) Arthur's Stone, the renowned cromlech on the summit of Cefn Bryn at Reynoldston, Gower (SS 491905). Legend tells us that it was a pebble that King Arthur plucked out of his shoe and threw here from Carmarthenshire.

(12) Coetan Arthur cromlech remains at Pont Fadog, Llanddwye-is-y Craig (SH 603228), is said to be a quoit which King Arthur threw from Moelfre Hill.

(13) Coetan Arthur, two cromlechs adjoining the school at Dyffryn Ardudwy in the Parish of Llanenddwyn, Gwynedd (SH 589228). These are said to have been thrown here by King Arthur from the top of Moelfre Hill.

(14) Maen Twrog, a standing stone in the churchyard of Maentwrog, Gwynedd (SH 664406), was thrown here from the top of Moelwyn Bach, 3 miles to the north, by St Twrog. The marks of his fingers and thumb can still be seen on the stone!

(15) The Devil's Quoit at Llanfihangel Rogiet in Monmouthshire (ST 439881) was hurled from Portishead across the Bristol Channel by the Devil in a fit of temper.

(16) Harold's Stones just outside the village of Trellech in Monmouthshire (SO 498052) were thrown to their present position by Jack o' Kent from the Holy Mountain (Skirrid Fawr) about 12 miles away.

(17) Maengwyn Hir near Crugelwin at Llanfrynach, Pembrokeshire (SN 238302), was thrown from the summit of Frenni Fawr by St Samson.

(18) Coetan Arthur, a rocking stone on the south slopes of Mynydd Preseli in the Parish of Mynachlog-ddu, Pembrokeshire (SN 135324), is said to have been hurled there by King Arthur from Dyffryn, 2 miles away.

(19) Llech y Tribed cromlech near Penlan at Moylgrove, Pembrokeshire (SN 101433) was hurled by St Samson from the summit of Carningli, Newport, Pembrokeshire.

(20) Caer Meini near Bedd Arthur in Mynachlog Ddu, Pembrokeshire (SN 142326), has an Altar Stone called Coetan Arthur which was thrown by King Arthur from Dyffryn, the farm near Gors Fawr Stone Circle.

Nine of these legends have some connection with King Arthur and four of them with St Samson, the Celtic saint who has no churches dedicated to him in Wales, although he spent time here before settling in Brittany.

Assorted Legends

Centuries ago, people who lived in the vicinity of these ancient megaliths made up stories to explain the presence and purpose of these puzzling features of the rural landscape. Over the course of time these stories became popular legends and the ones that have survived today are like the fairy stories that used to be told to children. They generally relate to giants and magical powers and are no longer taken seriously by anyone today.

A typical example is the story concerning three curious stones on Moelfre Hill, Caernarfonshire. Three women went to the top of the hill to winnow corn on Sunday, and a neighbour rebuked them for desecrating the Lord's Day. The women laughed and were turned into stone, which assumed the colours of the gowns they were wearing at that time. One was a dark red, one was white, and the third was a slate colour.

> *The apparently ridiculous nature of the tales has kept them alive over the centuries, and so today we have in much garbled form an account of landscape engineering thousands of years ago.*
>
> Janet and Colin Board

Some Fascinating Legends

The Lady Stone.

Pay your Respects to the Lady
Lady Stone, also known as Arglwydd's Stone, is 7 feet tall and said to resemble a woman wearing a cloak. There is a tradition that everyone who passes this way should tip their hat to the Lady Stone. It is also known as Black Horse Inn Stone and stands in a field belonging to Tremeini Farm.

Location: Beside the A487, 1 mile west of Dinas Cross, Pembrokeshire – SN 008388 (145)

Golden Grove Stone.

Once Thought to be of Druidic Origin

Golden Grove Stone, also known as the Druid's Altar, is about 4½ feet high and composed of limestone and square in shape. British antiquarians once believed that megalithic monuments were erected by the Druids. However, the megaliths antedate the Druids by at least 1,000 years. Yet it is quite likely that the Druids used megaliths as sites for their religious rituals. The naming of nearby Druidstone House also relates to the belief that this was once a site of Druidic activity.

Location: In a field above the River Grwyne, near Golden Grove Farm between Druid's Altar and the Dragon's Head Inn, Llangenny, Brecknockshire – SO 240178 (161)

Some Fascinating Legends

The Growing Stone.

It Just gets Taller and Taller!
The Growing Stone is the second tallest standing stone in Powys. It is composed of Old Red Sandstone and is about 13 feet high. There is a local tradition that it is impossible to accurately measure the height of this stone for it is constantly growing in size.

Location: At the entrance to the now disused Cwrt y Gollen army camp on the north side of the A40 between Abergavenny and Crickhowel, Brecknockshire – SO 232169 (161)

Maen Hir-y-maes Mochnant.

The Stone that Killed a Dragon!

Maen Hir-y-maes Mochnant is also known as Post Coch and Post y Wiber and a local story tells of a dragon or winged serpent which played havoc in the neighbourhood, destroying flocks of sheep and herds of cattle. Many plans were devised for the destruction of this monster, but they were all unsuccessful. However, a wise man came up with a strange plan. A large stone pillar was erected and studded with iron spikes. The colour red was believed to attract dragons so the pillar was carefully draped with a scarlet cloth, concealing the spikes. When the dragon next appeared, he spotted the red drapery and rushed towards it. The bright colour infuriated the creature and it beat itself against the pillar for many hours with the result that it died from exhaustion and loss of blood.

Location: Llanrhaedr yn Mochnant off the B4396, Montgomeryshire – 123260 (125)

Some Fascinating Legends

Maen Llog.

The Wishing Stone

Maen Llog is a large block of stone which is reputed to have been moved here from the abbey of Strata Marcella where the abbots were 'installed' on it as part of a well-established ritual. But after the Dissolution of the Monasteries, in the reign of King Henry VIII, it was brought to Welshpool and a new ritual established. Folk who were required to do penance were made to stand on the stone, dressed in a white sheet and, with a candle in one hand. However, the Puritan Vovasour Powell had the stone taken out of the church because he considered it to be an object of superstition.

When the stone was transferred to the churchyard, where it now stands, it was not long before it took on a new role, as a wishing stone. People would climb on to it and turn three times to face the sun and make their wish. It is not surprising that the stone is well polished from all this human activity.

Location: St Mary's Church, Welshpool, Montgomeryshire – SJ 225076 (126)

Carreg Lefn.

Once Believed to Mark Buried Treasure

Carreg Lefn (The Smooth Stone) is a massive standing stone 12 feet high, and sometimes referred to as Maen Press (The Brass Stone). At one time it was believed to stand near treasure held in a brass container which could be dug up by anyone who traces the shadow made by the stone at a particular time of the day.

Another story claims that if you can read an inscription on the stone, it will obligingly move to one side to reveal the treasure. Unfortunately there is no obvious inscription, but natural marks resembling one can be seen.

Location: Near Rhosgoch, Anglesey – SH 407903 (114)

Some Fascinating Legends

Carreg Lleidr – 'the Robber Stone'.

The Thief who was Turned into Stone

Carreg Lleidr is a strange looking standing stone which resembles a hump-backed man. It is called the Robber Stone by local people, who tell a story of a man who stole the Bible and Communion vessels of St Tyfrydog's Church and, whilst carrying them away on his shoulder, was suddenly turned into stone. On Christmas Eve when the clock strikes twelve the stone is said to run the field three times.

Location: In a field near St Tyfrydog's Church in the village of Llandyfrydog, 2 miles east of Llanerchymedd, Anglesey – SH 446843 (114).

The Druidstone.

Stones that go Drinking and Swimming

The second most popular legend associated with prehistoric standing stones in Wales is the one relating to the stone (or stones) going for a drink in a nearby river or pool.

A Stone that Likes to Drink when the Cock Crows
The Druidstone is also known as Gwal y Filiast (the greyhound bitch's lair). This impressive standing stone is 10 feet 6 inches high, 5 feet wide at the base and 3 feet thick. When a cock crows at midnight the stone is said to uproot itself and go down to the River Rhymney for a drink.

Location: In the private grounds of Druidstone House, St Mellons, Monmouthshire – ST 235836 (171)

Maen Llia.

It Goes for a Drink in the River Nedd
Maen Llia, a massive trapezoidal-shaped standing stone composed of Old Red Sandstone, is a prominent feature at the north end of the Llia Valley. A stile on the east side of the road provides access to the stone. Situated in a depression, probably caused by sheltering sheep, it stands at an altitude of 1,300 feet above sea level and points exactly north-south, in line with the valley, and was possibly erected to guide travellers across the hills between the Senni and Llia valleys.

It is 12 feet high, 9 feet in breadth and 2½ feet thick and used to show evidence of Latin inscriptions. These were mentioned by Macalister in 1922, who recorded that he saw the letters: ROVEV/S.... SOVI and VASSO, but these are no longer visible. There is a legend that the stone, on hearing the crowing of a cock, goes for a drink in the River Llia.

It is significant that on Midsummer Eve the sun casts a shadow of the stone downhill to reach the Afon Llia stream, about 230 feet away.

Location: Near Bryn Melyn, at the head of the Llia Valley, near Llethr on the Heol Senni to Ystradfellte road, Brecknockshire – SN 924192 (160)

The Four Stones of Old Radnor.

Four Thirsty Stones

Radnor Four Stones are glacial boulders which have been set up with their flat surfaces facing inwards. They are said to mark the burial place of four kings killed in battle nearby. Every night when they hear the bells of Old Radnor Church the stones are said to go down to Hindwell Pool for a drink.

The largest stone is 6 feet high and one to the south-west has three possible cup marks carved on it. A fifth stone may have been removed and taken to Old Radnor Church (about 1 mile away) to be carved into a font. It is of interest that about 5 miles west-south-west of the Four Stones is a boulder with thirty-two cup marks carved on it.

Location: Beside a minor road due south of Kinnerton, near Old Radnor, Radnorshire – SO 246608 (148)

Some Fascinating Legends

Dancing Stones

The Dancing Stones of Stackpole are three standing stones situated about 1 mile apart: Sampson Cross, Harold's Stone, and one at Stackpole Warren. They are said to get together occasionally and go down to Rhyd Sais (Saxon's Ford) to dance, and when tired they return to their individual sites. Sometimes, it is said, the Devil accompanies the Dancing Stones on his flute. If anyone witnesses the stones dancing then they will have exceptionally good luck.

Locations: Near Samson Farm (SM 962963), at Stackpole Warren (SM 984946) and in a field near The Home Farm (SM 968958 (158)), Pembrokeshire.

One of the Stackpole Dancing Stones.

Sleeping at a Megalithic Site

There is also a group of legends relating to sleeping at night under the capstone of a dolmen. The best known is one associated with Tinkinswood dolmen at St Nicholas in the Vale of Glamorgan (ST 082733). Anyone who sleeps within it on a 'spirit night' will suffer a calamity. He or she will either die, go raving mad or become a poet.

Lligwy Dolmen (or Arthur's Quoit) at Penrhos Lligwy in Anglesey has a story in which a fisherman fell asleep under it and dreamt that he rescued a beautiful maiden from the stormy sea. She turned out to be a witch and gave him a little golden ball containing a snakeskin charm, which he had to wash in the sea once a year.

Anyone who sleeps under Coetan Arthur near Llanfair Hall in the Parish of Llanfair-Is-Gaer in Gwynedd (SH 515660) through the night of St John's Festival will rise in the morning as strong as a giant or as weak as a dwarf.

The Men-an-Tol Stone.

A holed stone at Heston Brake Burial Chamber in Monmouthshire.

Healing Stones

Holed stones were widely believed to possess healing power. Such beliefs probably stem from the position of stones at the entrance to prehistoric burial chambers: a symbol of the birth passage in the ancient rites of initiation and rebirth.

The Men-an-Tol Stone near Morvah, Cornwall, is a good example. It is a wheel-shaped stone with a central hole about 2 feet in diameter and it stands upright between two standing stones. It is possible that the three stones were once part of a Neolithic burial chamber.

At one time children were passed naked three times through the hole to cure them of rickets. Adults seeking relief from rheumatism or spine troubles were told to crawl through the hole towards the sun nine times. This holed stone is also known as the Crick Stone due to the time when people suffering from a crick in the neck were allegedly cured by being passed three times through the opening.

10
Astronomical Significance

Looking at the evidence of megalithic man's fascination with astronomy, one gets the impression that it cannot have had just an abstract purpose; that, instead, it had a mystical yet practical significance.

Francis Hitching

The idea that certain stone circles were aligned to the Sun, Moon or stars dates back to the eighteenth century when William Stukeley noted in his book on Stonehenge that the stones were aligned to the Midsummer sunrise. It was the eminent English astronomer, Sir Norman Lockyer (1836–1900) who first gave scientific support to the idea that many megalithic sites have astronomical significance. He surveyed ancient sites throughout Britain and in Egypt and became convinced that the ancients had set up their stones to observe the Sun, Moon and certain stars for calendrical purposes. He proved that Stukeley had been correct and that the principal axis of Stonehenge is aligned with the angle of the Midsummer sunrise. It rises above the Heelstone, defining the straight avenue that runs from the centre towards the sunrise.

However, it was not until the 1960s that the relevance of these ancient sites to astronomy began to be taken really seriously. In 1965, Professor Gerald Hawkins published his book *Stonehenge Decoded* which detailed his investigations at this special megalithic site in which he found evidence to suggest significant solar and lunar alignments encoded in the relationships of the stones. Due to his work an image of Stonehenge as a sort of prehistoric computer emerged. It has even been suggested that it was built as an astronomical observatory for studying the motions of the Sun and the Moon.

Stonehenge has long been world-famous and in September 2014 immediately after the NATO summit in Newport SE Wales, President Obama, before flying back to America, made a special visit to Stonehenge for it was something that he had long wanted to see.

Some of the claims by Hawkins were hotly disputed by archaeologists and the challenge was then taken up by Alexander Thom of Kilmarnock, formerly Professor Emeritus of Engineering at Oxford University. He visited hundreds of British stone circles and made meticulous surveys, which showed that dozens of megalithic sites from the Outer Henrides to South Brittany were designed as lunar observatories and probably used for the accurate prediction of eclipses. His results were then linked with astronomical information relating back to prehistoric times and he concluded the following:

(1) The ground plans of the rings were accurate geometric constructions.

(2) A basic unit of measurement seemed to have been employed which he called the 'megalithic yard' of 2.72 feet (81.25 centimetres).

(3) Stone circles and certain single stones could have been used as backsights for observing astronomical phenomena.

(4) An eclipse would have been a moment of awesome significance.

> *To early man the eclipse of the sun or moon must have been an impressive spectacle, and a desire to master eclipse prediction probably motivated Megalithic man's preoccupation with lunar phenomena.*
>
> Professor Alexander Thom

> *As we uncover increasing evidence that ancient man was obsessively interested in the heavens, it seems clear that he had some instinctive rather than intellectual sense of the importance.*
>
> Colin Wilson

Astronomical Significance

An important site in Ireland which demonstrates an astronomical alignment is the Neolithic tomb at Newgrange, situated north-west of Dublin. It was built in about 3250 BC, about 500 years before the Pyramids of Egypt, and is therefore the oldest existing building in the world. Faced in quartz and surrounded by a huge circle with massive standing stones, it is a very impressive sight.

At the entrance to the mound is a horizontal stone carved with concentric circles, diamond shapes and multiple spirals. From there a 70-foot-long passage leads to the burial chamber, which measures 18 feet by 21 feet in plan and is decorated with carved designs of spirals and lozenges.

At the winter solstice from 19 December to 23 December the sun's rays shine through a slit in the roof box over the entrance, down the passage and for 17 minutes after dawn on midwinter day, illuminating the rear wall of the burial chamber. The triple spiral carving at the end of the chamber is thus lit up by the sun. It appears that Newgrange served as an astronomical clock that could be used for establishing the time of midwinter. Just outside the entrance is a large decorated kerbstone which displays a remarkable example of neolithic art. This monument was erected about 1,000 years before the circle of sarsen stones at Stonehenge.

Newgrange Neolithic tomb before excavation and restoration.

Megaliths of Wales: Mysterious Sites in the Landscape

Old photograph of the remains of Gwernvale Cromlech in Brecknockshire, which was partially destroyed when excavated by Sir Richard Colt Hoare in 1808.

II

The Destruction of Megalithic Monuments

The great tragedy of megalithic civilisation occurred when man lost touch with the spirit.

John Michell

A large number of Megalithic monuments have unfortunately disappeared during the passing centuries. Many have been destroyed through agricultural activities and road construction. A large number would also have been removed during early Christian times, for they were sometimes replaced with the building of a church. The early Christian fathers treated the ancient megaliths as idols of the pagans and caused the first deliberate damage and destruction of these ancient stones.

In the edict of Arles in AD 452 is the statement: 'If any infidel either lighted torches, or worshipped trees, fountains or stones, or neglected to destroy them, he should be found guilty of sacrilege.'

No record was made of the ones that were destroyed but one may surmise that some of them were replaced by church sites or wayside Christian crosses. Remains of ancient stones have been found in the older churches and some single standing stones have been cut into the shape of the so-called Latin cross used by the Western churches.

In the reign of William IV the Highway Act of 1835 empowered a road surveyor:

> ... to enter any waste land or common to dig and search for stone and remove the same. He may also take stones from any river. He may go into another parish and do as above, provided he leave sufficient stone for the said parish. He may enter enclosed land with the consent of the owner, and remove stone, paying nothing for the same, but paying for

any damage caused by transportation of the stone. If the owner refuses consent, the surveyor may apply to the nearest justice, who may authorise him to enter the enclosed land to remove any stone he requires.

In Victorian times, enthusiastic antiquaries took delight in opening up many of these ancient tombs to dig out pots, skulls, stone axes etc., leaving only a vestige of remains for modern archaeologists to examine.

Fortunately, today we have laws that protect our ancient monuments! In the past, however, farmers were probably pleased to have these large stone relics dynamited and cleared off their land. This would not only give them more space for cultivation but also discourage travellers from trespassing to inspect the curiosities.

An Attempt to Remove An Ancient Stone
A squat stone called the Langstone can be seen on private land in a field to the east of Langstone Court, Monmouthshire. It is composed of a conglomerate material and is just 2 feet high and 4½ feet square. The Gwent writer Fred Hando tells of a farm labourer who once told him of an attempt by a ploughman to remove this stone. A chain was attached to it, man and horses heaved and heaved, but the stone was unmovable, being set very deep in the ground.

Location: In a field to the east of Langstone Court, Monmouthshire – ST 380898 (171)

The Langstone.

The Destruction of Megalithic Monuments

The remains of Blaen Digedi stone circle.

Remains of a Stone Circle
A solitary stone on Hay Common, beside the mountain road which connects Capel-y-ffin and Hay-on-Wye, is about 4 feet 6 inches high. It was identified in 1970 as all that remains of Blaen Digedi stone circle, 98 feet in diameter, which once stood here. It would have been the largest known stone circle in South Wales.

Location: On Hay Common, below Hay Bluff in the Black Mountains, Brecknockshire – SO 239373 (9161)

Penbedw Stone Circle.

Remains of Another Stone Circle
Penbedw Stone Circle was once 120 feet in diameter and the remnants stand in the grounds of Penbedw Park, partially hidden under a clump of trees. There were originally eleven stones but only five stones, 3 feet to 5 feet high, remain standing. Trees have been planted to show where the missing stones once stood.

Location: 1 mile south of Nannerch on A541 About 5 miles from Mold and 8 miles from Denbigh, Flintshire – SJ 172679 (116)

Please Note: It is on private land but can be seen from a layby on the A541 (Mold – Denbigh road).

The Destruction of Megalithic Monuments

Examples of Megalithic Monuments Completely Destroyed

(1) In 1842 a circle of 41 stones was recorded on Bwlch Craigwen in the parish of Penmorfa, Gwynedd. It was oval in shape and measured 66 feet by 54 feet, but during the next seven years it was destroyed.

(2) On Mynydd y Gwyrd in Glamorgan a circle called Carn Lwyd was described in 1842 as a triple concentric circle with an extreme diameter of 65 feet. The medial ring lay 10 feet within this and at the centre was a circular area about 8 feet in diameter which may have been a cistfaen. Locally this circle was known as Yr Allor (The Altar), but it no longer exists.

(3) Fedw Circle, near Glascwm in Radnorshire, was once regarded as one of the finest stone circles in Wales. It stands on the highest point of a raised area of peaty land with the ground falling away in all directions. A plan of the circle published in 1805 in *Archaeologia Cambrensis* shows 27 stones in a true circle with 3 stones outside the circle and another 5 inside, making 35 stones altogether. Lieutenant Colonel Morgan visited the site in 1913 and removed stones from the circumference of the circle and also some which also stood outside (on account of their being obstacles to the plough), which were placed in groups in their present positions, and others were broken up.

(4) Hen Dre'r Stone Circle in the Rhondda Valley was in existence in 1912 and described as being nearly complete, with a pointer stone, but there is no sign of it today.

(5) Several circles have also been destroyed in the Preseli Mountains in Pembrokeshire. Dyffryn Syfnwg was mentioned in 1911 as having a diameter of 78 feet and an inner ring diameter of 40 feet and a central platform 1.5 feet to 2 feet high.

(6) At Eithbed in the parish of Maenclochog there were two circles situated about 100 yards apart. The first one had a diameter of 150 feet and the second one was 120 feet in diameter and surrounded by a circular litter of stones, which may have formed an inner ring. Three other circles once stood at Maenllwyd and Clyn Saithmaen but they also have vanished.

(7) In the parish of Cyffylliog in Gwynedd there used to be a ringwork 22 feet in diameter, which was known as Llys Frenhines, 'The Queen's Court'. A boulder called Cader y Frenhines (The Queen's Chair) was taken from there in 1804, and erected in Pool Park Ruthin. It resembles an armchair.

It is amazing how many Welsh prehistoric stone monuments still remain to be seen in whole or part when one considers that they were erected perhaps more than 5,000 years ago. These stone monuments must have served a very important purpose for the original builders and they would have been carefully protected, but as generation succeeded generation the secrets of their uses were lost. But the ancient stones were still held in veneration and not often damaged or destroyed by the local population. It would not have been until the coming of Christianity that the early Christian fathers treated these stones as the idols of pagans and caused the first deliberate damage and destruction of these megaliths. They left no records of the ones that were destroyed but we may surmise that some of them were replaced by church sites or wayside Christian crosses.

Then during the nineteenth century modern man lost his respect for these ancient stones, for he had no regard for an awkward block of old stone that could hinder the use of a commercial site and large numbers of these stones were no doubt uprooted and removed. A good example of one that was removed as recent as the 1950s is a cromlech in the parish of Talgarth, Powys, known as Croes Llechan (SO 167364) which stood on the right-hand side of the main road from Talgarth to Hay-on-Wye. It was marked as Croes-Llechau on the One Inch OS map of 1831.

The worst case of destruction of a stone circle is at the largest one in the world; namely the Avebury Stone Circle in Wiltshire, England. When Dr William Stukeley visited it in 1743, he listed seventy-two stones constituting the entire layout of the temple which covers about 22 acres. Most of the standing stones were demolished before 1820 and split up for use as building materials. Only 27 standing stones now remain on the circumference of the immense stone circle out of what had been well over 100 standing stones.

PART TWO

Alternative Archaeology

Archaeology is an art rather than a science – in that its 'facts' are not always capable of proof. Yet new ideas can be as unwelcomed by the profession as they are in other arts.

Guy Underwood

To appreciate this section of the book one needs an open mind, for it contains material that some writers would have omitted for fear of ridicule. David Cowan summed up this situation in 1999 when he commented: 'Britain has an ancient and powerful knowledge just waiting to be rediscovered by any able-bodied person, provided they are not imprisoned in the mental straitjacket which our science, for all its benefits, imposes upon its subjects.'

During the last three decades there has been a growing awareness of the importance of these ancient sites and their links with our distant ancestors who undoubtedly possessed a now forgotten knowledge, often termed, the 'ancient wisdom', which it would seem gave them the ability to identify and harness terrestial forces. Many people shake their heads and pour scorn on such ideas, while others are at least prepared to give them careful consideration.

Archaeologists are fierce and will tear to pieces one of their number who makes an insecure generalisation. An outsider can afford to take more risks.

P. J. Helm

Megaliths of Wales: Mysterious Sites in the Landscape

Stonehenge restored.

Stonehenge as it may have appeared after the final rebuilding about 1300 BC.

> *Circles along with other megalithic monuments were carefully sited in the landscape and have definite relationships with underground streams and energies, as well as special events in the heavens.*
>
> Ian Cooke

12

Ley Lines and Scemb Lines

With the coming of Christianity the site of many mark stones, 'temples', and pagan altars became the sites of Christian churches or churchyard crosses, and almost all these, if of ancient foundation, align on the straight tracks, as do crosses on the wayside.

Alfred Watkins, The Old Straight Track

The term 'Ley', meaning an alignment of sacred sites, was coined in the 1920s by Alfred Watkin. He first outlined his theories in a booklet called *Early British Trackways*. This was superseded by *The Old Straight Track*, which he published in 1925. He observed that many ancient sites such as mounds, moats, churches and other holy places were often aligned in straight line, which he called leys. Watkins considered that the markers in this network of alignments were the remnants of traders' routes laid down in the Neolithic period.

… imagine a fairy chain stretched from mountain peak to mountain peak, as far as the eye could reach, and paid out until it touched the 'high places' of the earth, at a number of ridges, banks and knolls. Then visualise a mound, circular earthwork, or clump of trees, planted on these high points, and in low points in the valley other mounds ringed round with water to be seen from a distance. Then great standing stones brought to mark the way at intervals, and on a bank leading up to a mountain ridge or down to a ford the track cut deep so as to form a guiding notch on the skyline as you come up. In a bwlch or mountain pass the road cut deeply at the highest place straight through the ridge to show as a notch afar off. Here and there and at two ends of the way, a beacon fire used to lay out the track. With ponds dug on the line, or streams banked up into 'flashes' to form reflecting points on the beacon track so that it might be checked when at least once a year the beacon was fired on the traditional day. All these works exactly on the sighting line.

The theories of Alfred Watkins have been investigated by many who have read his fascinating book and at the same time derided by others. Ley hunting has certainly become a popular activity and there are thousands of enthusiasts who tramp the British countryside seeking and examining possible alignments. It must be mentioned however, that the existence of ley lines is not recognised by orthodox science.

Alfred Watkins suggested that they might represent ancient trackways and he coined the word 'ley' for these alignments because many of the places on them have names ending in 'ley', 'leay', 'lee' or 'leigh'. Castles and early churches often appear on leys because many of them were built on the sites of ancient earthworks or megaliths.

He was convinced that straight lines could be drawn through most, if not all, of the prehistoric sites in any given area and came to the conclusion that these sites had once served as sighting points along the pre-Roman trackways of the countryside.

Alfred Watkins was a senior partner in a Hereford flour-milling firm, a Fellow of the Royal Photographic Society, the inventor of the exposure meter and President of the Woolhope Club in 1917. He died in 1935 at the age of eighty.

However, Watkins was not the first to take an interest in leys, for Colonel Johnson, the Director General of the Ordnance Survey observed in the 1880s that there were interesting alignments connected with Stonehenge that did not seem to have occurred by chance. He pointed out to two archaeologists in 1895 that it was possible to draw a straight line on the map between Stonehenge, Old Sarum, Salisbury Cathedral and Clearbury Ring.

An even earlier investigator was William Henry Black, who in the 1820s, a century before Alfred Watkins, had been identifying alignments all over Britain. Records of his research show that he was aware of leys even in France and Italy.

It is thought that ley lines transmit or receive energies of the globe and they have been described as the meridians of the Earth through which her life force flows. Intersections of these lines are 'power places' once revered and the 'pagan sanctuaries' were sometimes replaced with Christian churches in later times. Native cultures in the Americas call them 'Spirit Paths' and the Aborigines of Australia refer to them as 'Song Lines'. Yet the existence of these lines is not scientifically acknowledged!

Questions That Need Answers

(1) What is the likelihood that such alignments would occur through chance alone?
(2) Were the leys created artificially by Neolithic man for the transmission of earth energy in a similar way that pylons and cables transmit electricity today?
(3) Are the leys channels to convey the energy as it is received by our planet? Or are they marking a system to show where it flows?
(4) Did Megalithic Man control the terrestrial currents by manipulating solar power?
(5) Why do trees planted on a ley line grow much faster?
(6) Does ley energy cause spiral growth in tree trunks?
(7) Did the ancient people believe that the lines of energy were the Earth's life blood which made the land fertile?
(8) Do these lines of force become charged with a vital energy that was perhaps designed to fertilise the Earth? Was this prehistoric engineering carried out on a world wide scale? Is the Earth becoming barren because the fertilising force has been disturbed?
(9) Sometimes standing stones lean at angles. Was this deliberate, as in acupuncture where needles are placed at angles so that particular results can be achieved?

SCEMB LINES

Alfred Watkins never defines or restricted the kind of sites to be included in the alignments that he called Leys, nor did he put forward any realistic ideas for their purpose, with the result that his critics called his 'Ley Line System' fanciful and illogical.

John Williams, an Abergavenny solicitor and experienced dowser, invented the term SCEMB as an acronym for the five classes of prehistoric sites found on alignments with prehistoric standing stones. The sites include the following:

Stone circles, standing stones
Camps, cairn, or tumuli
Earthworks
Mounds or moats
Burial barrows or dolmens

All of these categories can be considered to have a pre-Christian date, being at least 2,000 years old, or are situated at places where there are reasonable indications of the presence of a much earlier site which can be dated to prehistoric times.

John Williams identified a number of recurring angles between SCEMB lines where they meet or cross. These angles include 23½ degrees and its multiples of 47, 70½, and 94 degrees. He called them 'solar angles' because 23½ degrees is the angle of the Earth's declination with the sun. The present solar (declination) angle of 23½ degrees has changed from about 24 degrees some 4,000 years ago.

Investigations carried out by John over a period of thirty years have shown that every recorded prehistoric stone monument is positioned on at least one of these SCEMB lines. This applies to over 4,200 of these sites, which he painstakingly indexed under countries, counties and parishes with Ordnance Survey reference numbers for the whole of the British Isles. This means that each one of these prehistoric standing stone sites is placed where the original builders put them, in direct alignment with at least two or more of the pre-Christian sites. This only applies to the stone monuments and may not apply to camps, carns, tumuli, earthworks, mounds or moats, although the majority of them are found on SCEMB lines.

Ley Lines and Scemb Lines

John describes his technique as follows:

These SCEMB lines can be easily checked on the One Inch or larger scale Ordnance Survey Maps for any part of Wales, preferably those on which there are marked a good number of prehistoric standing stone sites. The simple way to do this is to go through the map carefully square by square and underline prehistoric sites which are mostly shown in Gothic lettering on Ordnance Survey maps.

When this has been done, take a ruler, and using one of the prehistoric stone sites as a centre, slowly rotate the ruler until it is noted that there are two others of the marked prehistoric sites appearing along the edge of the ruler which indicates that they are in a direct alignment with the first site chosen as the centre. Draw a line along the edge of the ruler to join up these sites, each of which may be as much as 5 miles apart on the ground and then continue rotating the ruler the centre, stopping to mark any other alignment where two or more of the underlined sites show along the edge of the ruler at the same time indicating other sites in direct alignment, until a complete circle has been made about the original centre.

Now move the ruler to another point marked as a prehistoric site and repeat the process until a complete circle has been made this centre point. This should be repeated until all the prehistoric stone sites that are marked on the map have been used. Care should be taken to ensure that the alignments drawn on the map should pass through the marked site, for otherwise it should not be treated as a SCEMB line.

When you have finished marking alignments on an Ordnance Survey map in this manner, then you should find that there are a number of SCEMB lines which often meet or cross at certain points. Where this happens, you should measure the angles between the lines which meet or cross. It will be found that the angle of 23½ degrees, which is the angle of the Earth's declination to the Sun (which will be referred to as the Solar Angle), or its multiples of 47 degrees, 70½ degrees and 94 degrees occur more often than one would expect. The lines on the side of these angles should then be marked in red to their full length so that they stand out from the map and indicate any possible polar or solar connection of the alignments.

The angle of the Earth's declination to the sun varies slightly over a long period of time by about ½ a degree but 23½ degrees is regarded as a good average. It is an awkward angle which cannot be obtained by the simple division of any normal angle found in the basic geometric figures such as 90 degrees or 60 degrees. It can be found approximately by using a right-angled triangle where one of the sides is 9 and one is 4.

EXAMPLES OF SCEMB LINES IDENTIFIED BY JOHN WILLIAMS

LINE A No1. Line commences at Hanging Stone Dolmen between the crossroads at Sardis and Thurston in the Parish of Burton, Pembrokeshire (SM 972983), which is marked as Burial Chamber on Ordnance Survey map scale 1:50,000 and goes south through:

No. 2. An earthwork at Hundelton, Pembrokeshire, on the side of the main road, near Bowett (SM 969008), which is marked Earthwork on the above mentioned map and continues south through:

No. 3. A probable standing stone site at Yerbeston, which is on the road leading north from the church at St Petrox in the Parish of Stackpole Elidyr, Pembrokeshire (SR 968981). Yerbeston is marked on the above mentioned map. The line continues south and ends at:

No. 4. Harold Stone at The Home End Farm, Bosherton in the Parish of Stackpole, Elidyr, Pembrokeshire (SR 968958), which is marked Harold Stone on the above mentioned map. This is nearly 10 miles south of Hanging Stone Dolmen at Burton, and this parish name may be a corruption of Burstone or Bearstone, which might have been the name of the dolmen.

LINE B No. 1. Starts at the 8½ feet high standing stone near Carrog and N of the church at Llanfechell, Anglesey (SH 370916) and goes SE through:

No. 2. Maen Chwyf, sometimes called Arthur's Quoit at Llandyfrydog, Anglesey (SH 432857), on through to:

No. 3. Carreg Leidr, a 5 feet high menhir on a knoll near the church at Llandyfrydog, Anglesey (SH 447844) and ends at a:

No. 4. Large round earthwork on the S side of the main road between Rhos Owen and Treffos at Llansadwrn, Anglesey (SH 540757).

LINE C No. 1. Begins at the tumulus above Linney (SR 889969) and goes ENE through a:

No. 2. tumulus near Browslate at Warren, Pembrokeshire (SR 906972) and ends at a:

No. 3. probable standing stone site at Yerbeston, Stackpole, Elidyr, Pembrokeshire.

13

Dowsing the Earth Energies

> *Every megalithic site is over a centre or channel of the terrestrial current whose emanations are detected by the dowser's rod.*
>
> John Michell

Dowsing is an ancient practice whereby hidden water deep in the ground can be detected by means of the movement of a forked stick held between the hands. As the dowser crosses a waterline, the twig or metal rod in his hands seems to come alive, twisting and turning so much that it is difficult to retain a hold. The movement has been described as like a strong upward spiralling that is almost impossible to control or resist. It can even pull the forearm muscles so much that they ache afterwards.

A more finely tuned method is by using a pendulum, which is a weight on the end of a cord. The pendulum can be regarded as a receiver and a transmitter of energy, but the source of its knowledge is a mystery.

The earliest record of dowsing at a Welsh prehistoric standing stone occurs in the works of Alfred Watkins. In 1930 he visited the Four Stones at Walton, near Presteigne, Powys (SO 246608), with a local water diviner who claimed there were two underground streams at different levels crossing below the four stones.

In subsequent years other dowsers have had similar results and it is now believed by some that there are always two underground streams crossing at different levels below all single prehistoric standing stones, and they are usually believed to be 20 or more feet below the surface of the ground where the stone is standing.

If the dowsers are correct in only some cases of underground streams passing directly under these ancient upright stones, then it raises a number of questions. Were these large prehistoric stones placed in position where there were crossing streams of underground water or were the underground streams, in fact, diverted to cross beneath the stones?

Dowsers find that the underground streams do not seem to pass underneath the individual stones in a stone circle, but there do seem to be some streams which start inside a stone circle and below ground and pass out in between some of the individual stones on the diameter of the stone circle. When dowsers operate at dolmens they sometimes find that above the two crossing underground streams there is another stream which flows in a southerly direction.

When T. C. Lethbridge dowsed the Marry Maidens stone circle in Cornwall he claimed that when he held his dowsing pendulum in one hand and rested the other hand on one of the stones, he felt the stone tingle as if it were electrically charged, whilst the pendulum swung violently.

Bill Lewis, an Abergavenny man, spent many years dowsing the standing stones in his local area and came to the conclusion that a crossing of underground streams beneath each 'active' standing stone creates a small static electrical field. The stone amplifies this and the energy emerges from the ground and passes up the stone in the form of a spiral with seven coils. He found that the force varied and changed polarity with the lunar cycle.

Tom Graves confirmed Lewis' research and found that he could detect seven bands on most large standing stones and decided that these were 'tapping points into a spiral release of some kind of energy that moved up and down the stone, following the lunar cycle'. Whilst dowsing a stone in the Avebury circle in Wiltshire he had to jump back, sensing that he was about to encounter a discharge of energy.

John Williams, the Abergavenny dowser maintained that:

> Sensitive people like dowsers sometimes detect different kinds of vibrations or powers at these sites if they are in their original positions. These are difficult to define but it is thought that there are seven different kinds of power bands of which three operate below ground level and the other four can be ascertained by some people on the sides of these stones above the ground. It seems that the first five power or wavebands can be experienced on all prehistoric standing stones but the top two bands, numbers six and seven, can only be felt on taller standing stones, which are over 5 feet high.

The fifth wave band up from the bottom of the stone, which has been called spiral power, is the easiest one for an open-minded person to experience. Unfortunately many people, through modern scientific teaching, believe that these things are not possible and they make up their minds not to experience any reaction when it is explained to them how it is possible to contact this curious natural power. This is done by placing the palms of both hands on the face of the prehistoric standing stone at about 5 feet above the ground level on the north or east sides of the stone during the hours of daylight. If the hands are placed firmly against the stone, after a short while, a responsive person will experience a peculiar sensation of being pushed away from one side of the stone.

This strange spiral power pushes a person away from the standing stone either to the right or the left. If it pushes him away to the right and he the crosses over his hands and puts his palms flat on the face of the stone so that his hands swap over positions, then the spiral will act in a reverse direction and push him away to the left. This is something like reversing an electrical current and indicates that the movement of the person away from the face of the upright stone is caused by some kind of power and is not the result of the person's imagination.

It has been found that this spiral power waxes and wanes in a twenty-eight-day cycle so there are times when the spiral power is less effective than at others. At the end of the cycle the power is reversed so that it moves a person to the right on one day then twenty-eight days later it will move the same person to the left. Some people who experience this spiral power feel afraid of the unknown and just want to forget about it. Others, because of the variable factors mentioned above, think that they have been misled in some way because they may not be able to repeat the experience when the power potential has become low when approaching a changeover time.

A few dowsers can detect seven different power bands at these prehistoric standing stones but it seems that the top two power bands, numbered (for convenience) six and seven, are only found on the taller stones that are over 5 feet high. The seventh waveband seems to have some connection with ultraviolet light and can be contacted by some people when they touch the top of one of these taller stones with the fingertips of both hands.

Megaliths of Wales: Mysterious Sites in the Landscape

John Williams dowsing the 5th waveband and being pushed to one side.

John Williams experiencing a muscular contraction on dowsing the 7th waveband.

It would seem that standing stones act as amplifiers for natural currents of energy within the earth and it is significant that they have been found to have been placed where two or more underground streams cross. We must consider the possibility that Neolithic man was more sensitive to the forces and cycles of nature than people are today and that he had the ability to manipulate 'earth energy' by erecting standing stones. The question is what did these ancient people use this energy spiralling a stone for?

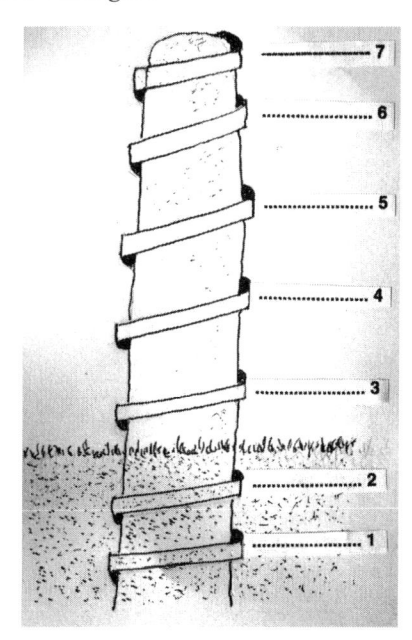

The Seven Power Bands.

Energy emerges from the ground and travels up the stone in the form of a spiral with seven coils. The megalith has the capacity to store and transmit energy.

Underground streams of water emit energy, which travels up the stone in the form of a spiral with seven coils.

There is evidence that the first five power or wavebands can be experienced on all prehistoric standing stones but the top two bands, numbers six and seven, can only be felt on the taller stones, which are over 5 feet high.

The fifth band affects the dowsers' balance and pushed them to one side.

The seventh band gives a tingling sensation like a mild electric shock, sometimes resulting in a violent reflex contraction of the back muscles.

It is of interest that there are seven important centres of energy vertically aligned in the centre of the human body close to the spine. These are known as chakras and they regulate the flow of energy through our energy system.

Seven is a mystical and important number which occurs frequently in nature. For example Isaac Newton identified seven colours of the rainbow: red, orange, yellow, green, blue, indigo and violet. There are seven visibly moving objects in the sky: Mercury, Venus, Jupiter, Moon and Sun. There are seven days in the week, seven notes on the musical scale: Do, Re, Mi, Fa, So, La, Ti, Do.

Richard Williams dowsing the 5th Band on the Great Oak Stone.

Dowsing the Great Oak Stone

This energy gathers strength as it rises up through the stone, and can frequently be felt physically as a tingling when touched with the fingertips, or as a loss of equilibrium if the palms of the hands are placed on the stone.

Francis Hitching

The Fifth Band

This band affects the dowser's balance and throws him to one side. The best time to feel the 5th waveband is on the day before New and Full Moon. Use a pendulum to find the position of the band by using your free hand as a pointer. Then place your hands flat on the surface of the stone and lean against it with your weight on your palms. It is essential to empty your mind and relax. Not everyone is pushed in the same direction and it will change according to the phases of the moon.

The spiral feeds energy from the ground to the sky during one half of the cycle and feeds from the sky to the ground during the other half. The bands on the stone seem to connect the stone into the flow of energy, apparently to control it. They seem to 'plug' the stone into energies both above and below ground, while the stone itself both works and is the right point through which the interchange of energies can take place.

Tom Graves

The Seventh Band

The dowser feels that the stone is moving and may feel a tingling sensation. A sudden release of stored energy can result in a violent reflex contraction of the back muscles. John Williams described the force as spiral-like, building up through the whole body and throwing the person touching it back from the stone.

He maintained that at the top of the stone there is a band of power that has something to do with the frequency of ultraviolet light. He could receive a physical sensation ranging from a slight prickling of the fingertips to a violent shock such as would be felt from a 12-volt car battery.

This amazing picture shows John Williams dowsing the 7th Band and it was taken at the exact moment that his fingers touched the top of the stone. The negatives on either side of this frame on the 35mm FP4 film were completely normal.

Operating at a very fast speed, the camera is capable of recording things that are not visible to the naked eye and sometimes strange patches or even shafts of light, caused by a concentration of ultraviolet light, appear on the exposed film. Is it a photograph of plasma energy?

Black-and-white film is best for showing up this phenomenon and it would seem that such film can pick up wavelengths that the human eye cannot see. The best results for these experiments occur on the day before a new moon and on days before a full moon, for then the energy is at its strongest.

John Williams dowsing the 7th Band.

Because human sensitivity is so limited, this energy is invisible to the normal human eye but can be recorded on sensitive film.

Remarkably, this spiral power waxes and wanes in a twenty-eight-day cycle and at the end of that time the polarity is reversed as a new cycle commences. Such forces of nature are as yet unrecognised by scientists but may well be attributed to electromagnetism. It is interesting that a standing stone near Avening in Gloucestershire is known as the 'Tingle Stone'.

Like all heavenly bodies, the earth is a giant magnet with a north pole and a south pole; the strength and direction of its currents are influenced by many factors including the proximity and relative positions of other spheres in the solar system, chiefly the sun and moon. Throughout the day, varying with their respective positions, they set up tides and currents within the terrestrial magnetic field.

It would seem that the earth's natural magnetism was not only known to men some thousands of years ago, but it provided them with a source of energy and inspiration to which their civilisation was tuned.

In the 1970s Bill Lewis, an Abergavenny electrical engineer and skilled dowser, accompanied by John Taylor, professor of Mathematics at King's College, London, visited the Llwyn-y-Fedwen Stone near Llangynidr (see page 13) and made an attempt to measure an electromagnetic force. They used an instrument called a 'goussmeter', which is used to measure static magnetic field strength. Also present was Dr Eduardo Balanovski, a young Argentinian physicist from Imperial College, London. When the meter was pointed at the stone, the needle reacted to indicate that the stone had an energy field that could be measured in bands the stone.

Dr Balanovski later commented: 'I do not personally believe that the stone was accidently chosen or accidently placed. The people who put it there knew about its power, even if they didn't know about electromagnetism.'

Bill Lewis maintained that there was experimental evidence which showed that the movement of water through a tunnel of earth, creates a small static electrical field and that the crossing of streams makes the field stronger. He believed that a stone placed immediately above the point where the streams cross acts in some way as an amplifier, despite the fact that there is no known theory of physics that can explain how this can happen.

Running water is a conductor of electricity, and in motion it generates a local magnetic field.

David D. Zinc

14
Fogging of Photographs

Fogging on photographs has been allied to the quartz composition of many standing stones or to the current transmitted by them.

Paul Screeton

Fogging on photographs of megalithic monuments is usually blamed on bad film or a camera leaking light, but when the negative frames of different subjects taken before or after the affected ones on the same roll of film are perfectly normal then it becomes obvious that it must be something to do with the stones themselves.

It proved of interest to check out a number of old books, published a century ago, containing early photographs of dolmens and standing stones to see if unusual patches of light have been captured by Victorian photographers using a plate camera. An example in which this occurs is in a rare book by J. E. Griffith, called *Portfolios of Photographs of the Cromlechs of Anglesey and Caernarvonshire* published in 1900.

On one photograph entitled 'Coetan Arthur Cromlech (W. View) near Caernarfon', which is in the parish of Llanfair-is-Gaer, Gwynedd (SH 515660), there is a clear patch of light at the bottom right of the huge capstone. It cannot be explained as sunlight judging from the position of shadows in other parts of the photograph and was perhaps caused by a concentration of ultraviolet light, which would not have been visible to the human eye.

Megaliths of Wales: Mysterious Sites in the Landscape

Picture taken *c.* 1900, showing fogging at Coetan Arthur cromlech.

Photographs that show these strange light effects are usually discarded and destroyed by the photographers who dismiss them as dud results and it is certainly rare for them to be included in a book. I had such problems myself when I first began to photograph standing stones in Monmouthshire and the Brecon Beacons National Park. It was very reassuring to me as a photographer when John Williams told me that he had experienced the same difficulties:

> I thought nothing of it for years and put it down to bad camera work; but in 1959 a friend and I photographed the same stone together. Both pictures came out with a fogged band across them in the same place. My picture was taken in colour and the lay band was dark blue. This led me to surmise that something in the stone was spoiling the pictures, a kind of ultra-violet light.
>
> Since then I have had many more examples of the same phenomenon. Most, if not all standing stones contain quartz, a crystal similar to that used with the cat's whisker in early wireless receivers. I believe most stones would show the fog effect if systematically photographed. I now think the stones form a gigantic power network, though I cannot guess for what purpose.

Fogging of Photographs

Fogging at the Llangybi Stone, Monmouthshire.

Strange fogging at Clynnog Cromech.

We tend to assume that a photograph is something without life, yet recent radiaetheric research has shown that the negative emulsion absorbs something of the psychic energy of whatever is photographed.

Muz Murray

Megaliths of Wales: Mysterious Sites in the Landscape

Powerful fogging at Clynnog Cromlech.

This cow seems to sense something that the human eye can not see.

15
The Significance of Quartz

The structure of quartz possibly converts earth currents. If quartz is linked to underground water-courses, a conversion from hydrostatic pressure into static electricity may occur.

Randall N. Baer and Viki V. Baer

It would seem that quartz was important to the megalith builders for there are many standing stones and circles that contain a large amount of this substance. Not all stones found in our rural landscape contain quartz, so one may infer that quartz was one of the necessary elements required in the stones chosen by the ancient erectors.

It is significant that in modern times there has been an increase the use of quartz crystals and silicon chips in the ever-expanding computer industry and projects relating to space research.

So what do we know about quartz?

Quartz, the most abundant mineral on the face of Earth, is a clear crystal that is usually colourless and is made up in a chemical form of one atom of the element silicon and two atoms of oxygen. It is given the chemical abbreviation SiO_2. The atoms forming any kind of recognised crystalline mineral are always arranged in certain patterns and these determine the structure and symmetry of the crystal. There are six main crystal systems and quartz belongs to the one called Hexagonal because the crystals have four different axes, of which three are equal and horizontal and make angles of 120 degrees with each other while the fourth and vertical axis is at right angles to the plane of the horizontal axis and is of a different length to the other three axis.

Crystals are classified as minerals in geological terms, but not all minerals are crystals – only those with a regular atomic structure forming a crystalline pattern. Quartz crystals are natural conductors of electromagnetic energy, which moves freely through the crystal's structure and is then projected out of its terminations.

Ultraviolet rays are able to pass through quartz uninterrupted and this is why many ultraviolet sunlamps have quartz tubes filled with mercury vapour to produce their sun-tanning rays.

In 1880, the famous French scientists Pierre and Jaques Curie, who discovered radium, were measuring the conductivity of quartz and they observed that the pressure on the testplates on which they were working produced a measurement on a sensitive electrometer. They had discovered what is now known as the piezolectric effect. This word is derived from the Greek *piezo* or *piezein*, which means to squeeze or press.

The mechanical pressure on a quartz crystal will produce a measurable voltage and conversely an electrical voltage applied to a crystal will produce a mechanical movement. It was found that, when alternating electrical current is passed through a crystal plate, the charges oscillate back and forth at the resonant frequency of the crystal.

Today, the vibrational properties of quartz crystals is recognised by science and they are used in watches, computers, radios and sonar technology amongst other things.

A sharp blow to a quartz crystal under pressure can cause thousands of volts of electricity to be discharged from it.

David D. Zink

16

Some Interesting and Intriguing Facts

It is amazing how many prehistoric megaliths still remain to be seen when one considers that they were erected perhaps more than 5,000 years ago. A large number have been destroyed through the passing centuries and the ones remaining probably only represent about 10 per cent of those that originally existed. There may well have been over 10,000 in Wales alone.

It has been estimated that there are more than 40,000 megalithic monuments still standing in Western Europe and Britain has more stone circles than any other country in the world. These open rings of erect stones are indigenous to the British Isles with no direct parallel on the European continent.

Between 4,000 and 6,000 years ago more than 1,000 stone circles and vast numbers of standing stones and dolmens were erected all over the British Isles, from the Shetland Islands in the north to the Isles of Scilly in the south-west of England and in most parts of Ireland.

An interesting question is, why was so much energy devoted to hewing great blocks of stone and transporting them sometimes many miles to be erected in a specially chosen place?

They Were Laid Out to A Plan

It would seem that megaliths were laid out to a fixed plan and erected by an intelligent people. In 1967, Alexander Thom, Professor Emeritus of Engineering Science at Oxford, published his research, having surveyed more than 600 megalithic sites in Britain and France. He concluded that prehistoric man had laid them out with astonishingly precise engineering and skill, in an astronomical alignment. He also discovered a basic unit of measurement: the megalithic yard of 2 feet 8⅝ inches (83 centimetres). It became apparent that the stones were erected by men who had a very considerable knowledge of geometry and astronomy.

It may be significant that certain stones have been placed at varying angles. The needles used in acupuncture are also placed at angles to produce the desired effect.

The Enigma of Electricity

(1) The Earth is surrounded by electrical fields and the two polar regions are like giant magnets that drive unseen currents around the globe.

(2) Electricity relies on polar magnetism, which is not generally recognised as a very important part of the everyday life of people who live in the modern-day Western culture. If there was no Polar Force, our lights would go out and a lot of machines would come to a grinding halt.

(3) Man may know all there is about harnessing the force, but electricity remains an enigma. If we touch something, see it, hear it or smell it then we are very much aware that it exists. But what about the invisible things such as radio waves or electricity? They certainly exist and modern science accepts them as fact.

(4) The theory is that electric current is a flow of electrons, minute particles far too small to see through any microscope. It takes a flow of billions of electrons to make even a small current.

(5) An electromagnetic wave is a wave of energy propagated in an electromagnetic field.

(6) The dowser Andrew Davidson, when investigating stone circles, has found that each stone is predominantly positive or negative and oppositely charged to its neighbour. The polarity changes six days after the new moon. On one occasion, he even experienced this change while he was dowsing a circle. His pendulum suddenly stopped turning and then began turning in the opposite direction.

Some Interesting and Intriguing Facts

Effects of the Sun and Moon

(1) The megalith builders had a considerable interest in eclipses. Many of the stones are aligned to the rising and setting of the sun on particular days of the year. Was this because the sun altered the nature of the earth current? An eclipse of the sun alters the nature of the earth's magnetic currents. An eclipse of the moon also effects the level of earth magnetism.

(2) Eclipses of the moon take place when the moon is cut off from the light of the sun by passing through the shadow of the Earth. They can only occur when the moon and the sun are in opposite directions in the sky, and this is the time of the month when the moon is full.

(3) The Moon is a satellite of the Earth and it follows its path us It is an average 238,900 miles away and this distance varies slightly because it follows an egg-shaped (elliptical) orbit the Earth.

(4) The earth keeps the moon in orbit by exerting a gravitational pull on it, but the moon also exerts a gravitational pull on the earth and this affects the tides.

(5) The full moon produces a marked increase in magnetic activity noon with a quiet period just before sunset.

(6) The pull of the sun also affects the tides, although at about half the strength. When the directions of the sun and the moon are at right angles (as when the moon's phase is first and last quarter), the gravitational pull opposes each other, and the tides are weaker than average.

(7) When the moon is closest to the earth, its gravitational pull is greatest, and if this happens at full moon, the full moon spring tides will be higher than normal. Higher than average tides are called spring tides and lower than average tides are called Neap tides.

The fact that the moon draws the earth's magnetic current and its underground waters, as well as the tides of the ocean, is one example of a link between astronomy and geology, such as is characteristic of megalithic sites.

John Michell

17
Assorted Theories

The ancient people who built the megalithic structures were clearly involved in something practical as well as sacred, and that practice gave them a very special, very mysterious relationship with the Earth.

Paul Devereux

Initial Erection of the Stones
The writer Francis Hitching has suggested that prehistoric man discovered by accident that a natural stone standing over a site where underground forces are trapped will emit a strange power. He then identified other similar locations and erected stones over them and thus the beginnings of a megalithic network was created.

Water moving through the earth creates a static electrical field and when two streams cross, the field is increased because water is a great conductor of electromagnetic energy. When a stone is placed over the top of this point of intersection then it acts as an amplifier.

Electromagnetism
In simple terms electromagnetic energy, generated by the Earth, is what we call direct current because it flows in one direction only. The Earth is like a giant magnet, because like a dynamo it spins and electricity is generated somewhere within its core. Well, that is the theory, but in reality the Earth's magnetic field remains a little understood phenomena.

Assorted Theories

There is a web of electromagnetic and high-frequency energy waves linking the sun, the planets and the moon. This disturbs the Earth's magnetism, causing it to flow in tides and currents. These vary with the time of day, the phases of the moon and other astronomical factors. The Earth itself is like a giant magnet, which is affected by the phases of the sun and the moon. Just as the sea is tidal, there is also an ebb and flow of the terrestrial current.

The sun imposes a daily rhythm modified by other influences including that of the lunar cycle, for the moon exerts the same influence upon this invisible flow as it does on the tides. The full moon produces a marked increase in magnetic activity noon with a quiet period just before sunset.

The Earth generates a magnetic field, which is created deep in the Earth's core, and it protects us from radiation from space.

The moon, as well as the sun, the planets and the nearest stars disturb the Earth's magnetism, causing it to flow in tides and currents.

It would seem that:

(1) A racing pigeon will lose its ability to navigate if a powerful magnet is attached to its head.
(2) Whales are thought to beach themselves when they encounter geomagnetic anomalies.
(3) Scientists have found that magnetic particles in human brain tissue strongly resemble the internal 'biological magnets' that bees, whales, salmon and pigeons use as a navigational aid.
(4) In one experiment, bees were monitored flying back and forth between two locations, where they gathered food. But when their 'biological magnets' were scrambled, they became confused and went astray.
(5) Experiments carried out with transistor radios held close to standing stones have shown that while tuned into medium radio wave lengths to receive certain radio stations, at particular spots there is a narrow beam or ray emitted from the stone, which causes interference.

Acupuncture

Could the well-being of the Earth itself be materially altered by stone acupuncture?

Ian Cooke

It was John Wheaton in the early 1970s who first suggested the idea of 'Earth Acupuncture'. Tom Graves further developed it and suggested that if we consider the Earth as a living being then its energy flows and sacred centres relate to the meridians and acupuncture points in the human body.

In his book *Needles of Stone*, Tom Graves advocates that there are channels of terrestrial energy running across the globe and that the stones are acupuncture points where the megalithic people inserted stones into the Earth. He believes that the megaliths act a little like acupuncture needles in the Earth's surface, maintaining and stimulating the flow of vital energy where it is needed.

Acupuncture originated in China and the principle is that the human body is traversed by flows of ch'i along lines known as 'meridians'. At intervals along these lines are found acupuncture points which are stimulated by the insertion of needles. The flow of life energy in the body along the meridians can thus be adjusted and balanced at chosen spots.

An acupuncturist stimulates or sedates the flow of energy in the meridian by inserting needles into the appropriate meridians at strategic acupuncture points. He thus seeks to harmonise and balance the energy body, encouraging the physical body to heal itself. Some people claim that the Earth has an energy body with energy flow lines similar to the acupuncture meridians in the human body.

The Chinese relate earth energies to the landscape and identify forces of yin and yang, (negative and positive), represented by the white tiger and the blue dragon, flowing in currents known as Ling Mei (dragon's veins) the countryside.

There are in the earth's crust two different, shall I say magnetic currents, the one male, the other female, the one positive, the other negative...

E. J. Eitel, 1873

Assorted Theories

The Earth Force

> *There exists a striking network of lines and subtle forces across Britain, and elsewhere on spaceship Earth, understood and marked in prehistoric times by men of wisdom and cosmic consciousness.*
>
> Paul Screeton

Many of the writers who have written books about megaliths believe that there is a hidden force that our distant ancestors knew and used, but through the passing of time such knowledge has been lost. It would seem that man was once in balance with the environment and attuned to the life force; he was aware of the importance of Earth's energy networks.

Perhaps the Earth force is a form of fertilizer, for experiments have shown that trees planted on a 'Ley Line' actually grow much faster. It is significant that in farming folklore, the phases of the moon are important in the planting, germination and harvesting of crops.

The concept of 'earth energy' is based on the idea that the earth itself is a living being permeated with a strange force – a force that waxes and wanes, possibly under the influence of the moon or other planets. The force seems to have polarity which can be defined as either 'positive' or 'negative'. Where these magnetic currents intersect is the point where standing stones and dolmens have been sited.

The Earth's magnetic field was probably much greater during the period of megalithic construction. What is left of the force is now fragmented for since the fifth century the magnetic field of the earth has been running down, increasingly so since 1670.

> *All I know is that there is some form of energy and I can detect it from the underground streams and particularly the stones.*
>
> Bill Lewis

Glossary of Terms

Alignment: Straight rows of standing stones.
Avenue: Two parallel rows of standing stones.
Barrow: Round or long mound of earth containing a chamber or burial and sometimes surrounded by a ditch.
Blind Spring: Dowser's term for a spring where water does not appear on the surface of the ground.
Cairn: Round or long mound of stones often covering a chamber or burial.
Capstone: Horizontal stone on top of a chamber or passage.
Carreg is used to describe smaller stones often found in Welsh stone circles.
Chambered cairn: Chamber tomb covered with stones.
Ch'i: The Chinese name for subtle energies in the landscape and the human body.
Cist: A small burial pit made of stone, often resembling a coffin.
Cromlech: The Welsh name for a dolmen.
Cupmarks: Cup-shaped depressions carved in a stone are thought by some to represent stars and thus to show the stellar orientation of megalithic sites.
Cup and ring marks: Concentric rings a cup mark.
Cursus: A linear landscape feature, dating from Neolithic times.
Dolmen: Megalithic burial chamber with three or more uprights supporting at least one capstone.
Dowsing: A means of detecting subtle energies by the movement of a rod or pendulum held in the hand.
Earth Energies: The life force system of our Earth – the equivalent to the human body's acupuncture meridians.

Glossary of Terms

Equinox: The time when the Sun crosses the Equator making the night equal in length to the day.

Feng Shui: A Chinese system which recognises energy flows and forms in the landscape. Fen = wind, Shui = water and it means to live in harmony and peace with the land. There are no megalithic monuments in China.

Gaia: Some writers see the Earth as a living thing and give it the name of the Greek goddess Gaia.

Gallery grave: Rectangular megalithic burial chamber reached by a stone built passage, often with side chambers leading off it.

Geomancy: The art of designing and placing structures in the landscape so that the Earth energies enhance their intended use.

Henge: A non-defensive circular earthwork with a bank and ditch and one or more entrances, apparently used for ceremonial purposes during the late Neolithic period.

Ley Lines: Alignments of ancient sites in the landscape, between which trackways are supposed to run. This idea was put forward by Alfred Watkins, author of *The Straight Track*, published in 1925.

Logan Stones: Large stones that are critically balanced and may be rocked when a slight pressure is applied at a certain point. Consequently they are also known as Rocking Stones.

Long Barrows: These date from the Early and Middle Neolithic period, while Round Barrows were usually constructed later, during the Bronze Age.

Major Axis: The most significant alignment of a sacred site. *Minor Axis*: Any significant line drawn perpendicular to the major axis of a sacred site.

Megalith: This term comes from the Greek – mega (big) and lithos (stone) – and it refers to large stones or monuments built of them.

Megalithic Yard: By analysing distances in stone circles, the surveyor Alexander Thom identified a unit of measure, of 2.72ft, which he called the 'megalithic yard'.

Menhir: Breton term for a single standing stone. Men means stone and hir means long. *Maen hir* is Welsh for 'long stone'.

Mound: Pile of earth and stones covering a burial chamber or deposit.

Neolithic: The latter part of the Stone Age, when most megaliths were constructed.

Portal Stone: The stone at the front or entrance to a chambered tomb.

Primary Water: Created in the bowels of the earth as a biproduct of various chemical reactions. It does not come from rain water that has soaked into the Earth.

Recumbent stone: A large stone lying horizontally between two others still standing.

SCEMB: An acronym for the five classes of prehistoric sites found on alignments with prehistoric standing stones. The sites include: stone circles, standing stones, camps, cairns earthworks and mounds.

Solar Angles: These are angles of 23½ degrees, which is the angle of the Earth's declination to the sun, or multiples thereof.

Solstice: The times when the Sun reaches its maximum distance from the Equator. Summer Solstice (21st June) occurs when it reaches the Tropic of Cancer; Winter Solstice, when it reaches the Tropic of Capricorn.

Standing Stone: A solitary stone erected in prehistoric times.

Stone Circle: A ring (not always circular) of standing stones.

Stone Row: A line of standing stones running for various distances across the countryside and they probably date from the Bronze Age.

Telluric Force: A term, largely used by dowsers, for earth energy. It is inspired by the name of the Roman earth goddess Tellus.

Yang: Active, Positive (+) polarity.

Yin: Receptive, Negative (-) polarity.

Further Reading

Atkinson, R.J.C., *Stonehenge*, (Hamish Hamilton, 1956)
Barber, Chris, *Mysterious Wales*, (David & Charles, 1982 and Paladin, 1983)
Barber, Chris and Williams, John, *The Ancient Stones of Wales*, (Blorenge Books, 1989)
Bord, Janet and Colin, *Mysterious Britain*, (Garnstone Press, 1972)
Ibid., *The Secret Country*, (Elek Books 1976)
Ibid., *A Guide to Ancient Sites in Britain*, (Paladin, 1971)
Burl, Aubrey, *Prehistoric Stone Circles*, (Shire, 1977)
Cowan, David and Silk, Anne, *Ancient Energies of the Earth*, (Thorsons, 1999)
Devereux, Paul and Pennick, Nigel, *Lines on the Landscape*, (Robert Hale, 1989)
Gaynor, Frances, *The First Stonehenge*, (Christopher Davies, 1986)
Graves, Tom, *The Diviner's Handbook*, (Destiny Books, 1990)
Ibid., *Dowsing*, (Turnstone Press, 1976)
Ibid., *Needles of Stone*, (Turnstone Press, 1978)
Grimes, W.F. *The Megalithic Monuments of Wales* (National Museum of Wales, 1936)
Grinsell, L.V., *Folklore of Prehitoric Sites in Britain* (David & Charles, 1976)
Hawkins, G.S., *Stonehenge Decoded*, (Souvenir Press, 1966)
Headingham, Evan, *Ancient Carvings in Britain*, (Garnstone Press, 1974)
Helm, P.J., *Exploring Prehistoric England*, (Robert Hale, 1971)
Hitching, Francis, *Earth Magic*, (Cassell, 1976)
Lethbridge, T.C., *The Legend of the Sons of God*, (Routledge & Kegan Paul, 1972)
Ibid., *The Power of the Pendulum*, (Arkana, 1976)
MacKie, Ewyan W., *The Megalith Builders*, (Phaidon Press, 1977)
Michell, John, *The View over Atlantis*, (Garnstone Press, 1973)
Ibid., *The Earth Spirit*, (Thames & Hudson, 1975)
Ibid., *A Little History of Astro-Archaeology*, (Thames & Hudson, 1977)
Millar, Hamish and Broadhurst, Paul, *The Sun and the Serpent*, (Pendragon Press, 1989)
Robins, Don, *Circles of Stone*, (Souvenir Press, 1985)
Screeton, Paul, *Quicksilver Heritage*, (Thornsons, 1974)
Thom, Alexander, *Megalithic Sites in Britain*, (Oxford University Press, 1967)
Ibid., *Megalithic Lunar Observatories*, (Oxford University Press, 1971)
Underwood, Guy, *The Pattern of the Past*, (Museum Press, 1969)
Watkins, Alfred, *The Old Straight Track*, (Methuen, 1925, Abacus, 1974)
Wood, John Edwin, *Sun, Moon and Standing Stones*, (Oxford University Press, 1978)

Other Books by Chris Barber

Walks in the Brecon Beacons (1976)
Exploring the Waterfall Country (1976)
Exploring Gwent (1984)
Ghosts of Wales (1979)
Mysterious Wales (1982/ 2000)
Cordell Country (1985)
The Romance of the Welsh Mountains (1986)
More Mysterious Wales (1986)
Hando's Gwent –Volume 1 (1987) and Volume II (1989)
The Ancient Stones of Wales (with John Williams, 1989)
The Seven Hills of Abergavenny (1992)
*Journey to Avalon (*with David Pykitt, 1993 and 1997)
Portraits of the Past (with Michael Blackmore, 1996)
In Search of Owain Glyndwr (1998 and 2004)
Eastern Valley: The Story of Torfaen (1999)
Exploring Blaenavon Industrial Landscape World Heritage Site (2002)
Exploring Kilvert Country (2003)
Llanover Country (2004)
In the Footsteps of Alexander Cordell (2007)
40 Classic Walks in the Brecon Beacons National Park (2009)
Arthurian Caerleon (1996 and 2010)
Abergavenny: Historic Market Town (2011)
Exploring Hill's Tramroad (2012)
King Arthur: The Mystery Unravelled (2016)
Mysterious Wales (new edition, 2016)